CHARACTER PEOPLE

Also by
Alfred E. Twomey and Arthur F. McClure
THE VERSATILES

Also by
Ken D. Jones, Arthur F. McClure, and Alfred E. Twomey
FILMS OF JAMES STEWART

CHARACTER PEOPLE

Ken D. Jones, Arthur F. McClure,
and Alfred E. Twomey

SOUTH BRUNSWICK AND NEW YORK: A. S. BARNES AND COMPANY
LONDON: THOMAS YOSELOFF LTD

A. S. Barnes and Co., Inc.
Cranbury, New Jersey 08512

Thomas Yoseloff Ltd
108 New Bond Street
London W1Y OQX, England

Library of Congress Cataloging in Publication Data

Jones, Ken D.
   Character people.

      Includes index.
      1. Moving-picture actors and actresses—Biography.
I. McClure, Arthur F., joint author.
II. Twomey, Alfred E., joint author. III. Title.
PN1998.A2J6   791.43'028'0922 [B]   74-30972
ISBN 0-498-01697-8

For—

Cliff and Clifton Jones
John and Vera Twomey
Art and Helen McClure

Who loved and encouraged us—

Printed in the United States of America

Contents

JOHN FIEDLER	77	CHARLES KEMPER	115
EDWARD FIELDING	78	CLAUDE KING	115
STANLEY FIELDS	79	WERNER KLEMPERER	115
JAMES FINLAYSON	80	FRED KOHLER SR.	116
PAT FLAHERTY	81	ALMA KRUGER	117
JOE FLYNN	83	HENRY KULKY	118
WALLACE FORD	83	JOHN LARKIN	118
WILLIAM FRAWLEY	83	JACK LARUE	118
BERT FREED	84	LUCILLE LAVERNE	120
DWIGHT FRYE	85	IVAN LEBEDEFF	121
RICHARD (SKEETS) GALLAGHER	86	GEORGE J. LEWIS	122
CLAUDE GILLINGWATER	86	DORIS LLOYD	122
LUCILE GLEASON	86	JAMES (JIMMY) LYDON	122
BILL GOODWIN	88	WILLIAM H. LYNN	124
LEO GORCEY	88	MERCEDES MCCAMBRIDGE	124
WILLIAM GOULD	90	KENNETH MACDONALD	126
ALEXANDER GRANACH	91	WILBUR MACK	126
HARRISON GREENE	91	MALA	127
DABS GREER	91	HANK MANN	128
HUNTZ HALL	91	GEORGE MARION	129
JOHN HALLIDAY	93	JOHN MARLEY	131
KENNETH HARLAN	94	TULLY MARSHALL	131
OTIS HARLAN	95	MARION MARTIN	132
PAUL HARTMAN	95	STROTHER MARTIN	133
RONDO HATTON	95	PAUL MAXEY	134
SESSUE HAYAKAWA	96	MYRON MCCORMICK	135
VINTON HAYWORTH	99	GEORGE MCKAY	135
MYRON HEALEY	99	EDWARD MCNAMARA	135
TED HEALY	99	HOWARD MCNEAR	136
EILEEN HECKART	101	BUTTERFLY MCQUEEN	139
O.P. HEGGIE	101	PATRICK MCVEY	139
HOWARD HICKMAN	101	EDWARD MCWADE	139
WILLIAM HOPPER	104	ROBERT MCWADE	140
ARTHUR HOUSMAN	104	ADOLPHE MENJOU	142
SHEMP HOWARD	104	BERYL MERCER	143
WALTER HUSTON	106	CHARLES MEREDITH	144
JACK INGRAM	106	PHILIP MERIVALE	145
ROSALIND IVAN	107	ROBERT MIDDLEMASS	146
BUD JAMISON	107	SILVIO MINCIOTTI	147
SOLEDAD JIMINEZ	108	GEORGE MITCHELL	148
HENRY JONES	109	MILLARD MITCHELL	148
NICHOLAS JOY	109	MANTAN MORELAND	149
CHARLES JUDELS	110	FRANK MORGAN	149
IAN KEITH	111	ADRIAN MORRIS	150
DEFOREST KELLEY	112	MAURICE MOSCOVITCH	151
LEW KELLY	113	CHARLIE MURRAY	152
PERT KELTON	113	BURT MUSTIN	153

CARROLL O'CONNOR	155	NATALIE SCHAFER	180
PAT O'MALLEY	155	WILLIAM SCHALLERT	180
BUD OSBORNE	155	VICTOR SEN YUNG	183
MICHAEL O'SHEA	157	GUSTAV VON SEYFFERTITZ	184
CECIL PARKER	158	GEORGE SIDNEY	184
ALICE PEARCE	159	ART SMITH	186
JOE PENNER	160	KENT SMITH	187
OSGOOD PERKINS	160	OLAN SOULÉ	189
NEHEMIAH PERSOFF	162	ARTHUR SPACE	189
HOWARD A. PETRIE	163	HOPE SUMMERS	190
JOHN PHILLIBER	164	CARL (ALFALFA) SWITZER	190
IRVING PICHEL	165	WILLIAM TALMAN	192
FRANCIS PIERLOT	166	ERNEST TORRENCE	192
CAMERON PRUD' HOMME	167	JOSEPH TURKEL	195
DICK PURCELL	167	LEE VAN CLEEF	195
CHIPS RAFFERTY	167	HAROLD VERMILYEA	196
FORD RAINEY	168	CHARLES WAGENHEIM	197
ISABEL RANDOLPH	170	RAY WALSTON	199
HERBERT RAWLINSON	171	BRYANT WASHBURN	199
GEORGE REGAS	171	ROBERT WATSON	200
CRAIG REYNOLDS	171	LEON "ABNER" WEAVER	200
JASON ROBARDS SR.	173	JAMES WESTERFIELD	203
BILL "BOJANGLES" ROBINSON	175	NYDIA WESTMAN	203
HAYDEN RORKE	175	BERT WHEELER	204
ANTHONY ROSS	176	SIR DONALD WOLFIT	205
DAME MARGARET RUTHERFORD	177	LOUIS WOLHEIM	207
BASIL RUYSDAEL	178	MONTY WOOLLEY	208
IRENE RYAN	179	JOE YULE	209
HOWARD ST. JOHN	180		

Preface

In this book we have attempted to rescue a part of the artistic achievements of the "character people" in the American motion picture. Almost certainly some critic will label our effort a "nonbook." We make no apologies, however, and offer this book to readers who share in our admiration for these overlooked professional actors who often labored in an unfair anonymity. The effects of their participation in the American film for more than four decades speaks for itself.

We have had the intelligent assistance of many people, but particularly Roseann Gargotta, Diana Cole, and Marsha Bird. We had the extraordinary efforts of Bruce Sarver, whose material on the career of Isabel Withers was most useful. Our indebtedness to Gloria and Roland Dykes, Clyde Crump, and Julien Yoseloff and the editorial staff of A. S. Barnes and Co. Inc., would be hard to overstate. We also owe a debt of gratitude to Nancy Jones and Judy McClure, who are consistently willing to support with great patience any adventure in scholarship.

Finally, we have been guided by the principle that as historians we should be concerned with breaking through the formalism of written history and record a distinctive aspect of American experience.

Introduction

When the authors researched and published an earlier volume, *The Versatiles: A Study of Supporting Actors and Actresses in the American Motion Picture, 1930-1955* in 1969, the public response was gratifying. Reviewers and individual readers responded positively to the book's acknowledgment of these fine players and their importance to the content of the American motion picture. Now, nearly five years later, we realize with a pang of sadness how many of these "character people" are no longer with us.

For several years, we have contemplated a sequel to this earlier book. The temptation to entitle our present study *The Son of the Versatiles* or *The Versatiles Rides Again* has been overwhelming at times and we have jokingly referred to this volume by those names.

How often did an average Saturday matinee or leaden thriller take on a human quality when a certain face (what *was* her name?) made her entrance? Often, the magic was enhanced by a simple shrug, a grin or a pop-eyed stare, but were delightful bridges between one major dramatic incident and another. Stars were often interchangeable, but once a character actor established himself as a certain type, audiences would not accept a metamorphosis. Ironically, many character people came out of stock companies trained to versatility. Gifted, serious actors, they often worked arduously to perfect even the most minute gesture. Good cops, cynical cabbies, wisecracking blondes abounded.

To those who are still active in films and television, we are as glad to see them almost as much as old friends. When we wrote to veteran character actor, Eduard Franz, his reply included his thanks for an interest and the observation that "what you are doing should have been done a long time ago." We agree that the recognition has come late. But not too late for the mention that they so richly deserve.

Actors and actresses like Charles Halton, Grant Mitchell, Donald Meek, Roscoe Ates, John Qualen, Frank Puglia, Eduard Franz, Arthur O'Connell, Bill Quinn, Reta Shaw, and Isabel Withers together represent a good cross section of the character actor, and also point up the difficulty in classifying them.

In undertaking this project the authors again faced the problem of selection in trying to determine the fine line between featured and supporting players and those who later became stars either on the stage, in films or on television. For example, Eduard Franz and Arthur O'Connell have achieved great popularity during other stages of their careers. So has Reta Shaw. Isabel Withers, on the other hand, labored for many years in relative anonymity. Bill Quinn had a long career in radio before entering films, and a parallel career in television over the past twenty-five years. But they were and are all character people. And proud of it. A review of their separate careers indicates the rich diversity of their backgrounds.

With two Academy Award nominations and a list of top stage, television and screen credits to his

Arthur O'Connell in _Follow That Dream_.

record, Arthur O'Connell has to be considered one of the best character actors in the theatrical profession. Although he has become famous because of his film career, he remains a character actor.

The versatile and unassuming performer has co-starred with many of the top names in pictures including: Jimmy Stewart, Bette Davis, Glenn Ford, Jack Lemmon, Marilyn Monroe, Lee Remick, Tony Curtis, Marlene Dietrich, and William Holden, to mention a few.

Prior to his concentration on a film career in the mid-1950s, O'Connell won the Antoinette Perry and Daniel Blum awards for his Broadway stage performance in the William Inge play, _Picnic_. It was his screen reenactment of his _Picnic_ role which won him the first Oscar nomination for Best Supporting Actor in 1955. His second, in 1959, was for his performance in _Anatomy of a Murder_.

Although he was termed an "overnight success" by some observers, O'Connell came up the slow, hard way. With a background of fifteen years in the legitmate theatre, it was not until his moving stage performance as "Howard Bevans," the reluctant suitor in the stage production of _Picnic_ won him raves, the film role opposite Rosalind Russell and

the nomination, that his career really went into high. Since his second Oscar nomination for his portrayal as "Parnell McCarthy," the country lawyer in _Anatomy of a Murder_, O'Connell has been able to pick and choose his roles.

Born in New York City on March 29, 1908, the youngest of four children of Michael O'Connell and Julia Byrne O'Connell, Arthur was sent to live with his aunt, Mrs. Charles Koetzner, at age two, when his father died. His mother, a practical nurse, had to work, so she kept only her eldest child with her until she died, when O'Connell was twelve.

He was graduated with honors from St. Michael's Grammar School, Flushing, Long Island, St. John's High School, and won a scholarship to St. John's College, Brooklyn. Although he was holding down several odd jobs to help pay his expenses, he participated in numerous school activities, and was captain of the debating team.

After he was graduated he worked briefly in the engineering department of the New York Edison Company and as a salesman at R.H. Macy in New York, but failed to find the excitement he hoped for in the business world. He then took a job as a door-to-door magazine salesman, and plied his wares in several states.

While selling magazines in Pittsfield, Massachusetts, he ran into an old friend, Helen Leatherwood. She was in show business, and the next day so was Arthur O'Connell.

He had accompanied her on a round of agents' offices, was mistaken for an actor, and offered a role in _The Patsy_, with the Franklin Park Stock Company, at Dorchester, Massachusetts. Although he made up to $110.00 a week as a magazine salesman, he took the offer when they gradually upped it from forty-five to ninety dollars a week.

In the 1930s, after working with various good, bad, and indifferent stock companies from one end of America to the other and spending six years in vaudeville, first in the famous sketch, _The Family Upstairs_, and then as a stooge for some of vaudeville's great comics—Bert Lahr, Bert Walton, and Roy Sedley—O'Connell was tagged for the role of Pepper White, the punch-drunk fighter in the road company of _Golden Boy_.

When _Golden Boy_ closed in this country, O'Connell went to England and played the same part in the Group Theatre's production produced by Robert Goldstein at the St. James Theatre. Arthur O'Connell was sure he had finally gotten into a

Arthur O'Connell in *Follow That Dream*.

successful play which would have a long run, but it was not to be. The play closed suddenly in the midst of the Munich crisis—and again O'Connell found himself out of work.

O'Connell persuaded an English movie producer to give him his first film assignment in *Murder in Soho*. Then he was featured in the London stage musical, *Bobby Get Your Gun*, with Bobby Hawes. Later, Associated British Pictures (the producers of *Murder in Soho*), offered him a better part in a picture, *The Luck of the Navy*, and a three-year contract. But this was 1939 and the American Embassy was requesting all Americans leave England and return home. O'Connell arrived in Manhattan one week before World War II broke out in Europe. He gathered up all his belongings and headed for Hollywood—fascinated with the idea of being a motion picture actor. But the only work he could find was in comedy shorts at R.K.O. with Leon

Erroll and Edgar Kennedy. Finally, Orson Welles hired him and he appeared in *Citizen Kane*. He played small parts in good pictures and big parts in bad pictures until he was signed for a top supporting role in *The Pride of the Yankees*. But on the day he was to report for work in this important film, he was drafted—nine months before Pearl Harbor.

After a year's study in an Army Service School at Fort Monmouth, he was assigned as an instructor at West Point where he taught classes in VHF (Very High Frequency) until he was summoned to New York to direct and act in *The Army Play by Play*, a series of one-act plays written, directed and acted by soldiers and employing the services of a different top female star each night.

That chore completed, he was assigned to Astoria to make Army training films until he was discharged in 1945.

After the war, O'Connell directed *Brighten the*

Corner, by John Cecil Holm, starring Charles Butterworth. Although he received good notices for his direction, he could not resist the opportunity to play Shakespeare. He joined Margaret Webster's repertory company and toured some thirty-six thousand miles in a Greyhound bus, playing Polonius in *Hamlet* and Banquo in *Macbeth*.

In telling about the lean years before *Picnic*, O'Connell remembers that in one season he appeared in five plays—by the world's top playwrights: Paul Vincent Carroll's *Chuckeyhead Story*, Clare Booth Luce's *Child of the Morning*, Donald Ogden Stewart's *The Kidders*, a revival of Eugene O'Neills's *Anna Christie*, and the American National Theatre and Academy's revival of *Golden Boy*—in which he again played Pepper White—all were failures. The longest run was *Golden Boy*, which opened at the Guild Theatre for ANTA and ran for six weeks.

In the 1950s, he met Kansas playwright William Inge, who wrote *Picnic* and it was his Broadway and film appearances in *Picnic* that turned the tide for him. His first Oscar nomination gave him not only bigger roles, but the chance to interpret roles as he felt them.

O'Connell never had an acting lesson until after he had been acting for fourteen years. Then, after she had turned him down four times, Mme. Maria Ouspenskaya relented her rule that she preferred to teach novices, and accepted when he had planked down fifteen hundred dollars, and with tears in his eyes, begged her to accept him as a pupil. "It was worth every dollar of the fifteen hundred dollars," O'Connell recalls, "because she taught me how to study, how to analyze, and how to prepare for a role—the homework every actor must do before essaying any role."

In 1961 he did his first television series, "The Second Hundred Years." He spent twenty-two days in South Viet Nam and five days in Thailand with the American soldiers during the Tet offensive in 1968. Upon his return he phoned the parents and families of 250 soldiers from California with whom he had spoken while in Southeast Asia—relaying personal news from the battlefront to those awaiting their return to the United States. The reactions to these personal telephone calls ranged from the almost unreal poignancy to the deeply touching gratitude of the recipients, the preponderance of the reactions leaning heavily upon the latter. "This," recalls O'Connell, "was the most reward-ing experience I have ever had—not only as an actor, but as a human being; to be with such great men even for such a short time.

Some of O'Connell's film credits since his first Oscar nomination include: *Solid Gold Cadillac*; *The Man in the Gray Flannel Suit*; *The Proud Ones*; *Bus Stop*; *April Love*; *Hound Dog Man*; *Misty*; *The Great Race*; *Your Cheatin' Heart*; *Operation Mad-Ball*; *The Anatomy of a Murder*, Academy nomination; *The Violators*; *The Monte Carlo Story*; *Pocketful of Miracles*; *The Third Day*; *Operation Petticoat*; *Cimarron*; *Follow That Dream*; *Voice in the Mirror*; *Merlin Jones*; *Law of the Jungle*; *Nightmare in the Sun*; *Gidget*; *A Thunder of Drums*; *The Great Imposter*; *Man of the West*; *Seven Faces of Dr. Lao*; *Kissin' Cousins*; *The Monkey's Uncle*; *Fantastic Voyage*; *The Birds Do It*; *The Silencers*; *The Power*; *The Reluctant Astronaut*; *Suppose They Gave a War and Nobody Came*; *There Was a Crooked Man*; *The Last Valley*; *They Only Kill Their Masters*; *Wicked, Wicked*; *Ben*; *Taste of Evil*; and *Huckleberry Finn*.

Concerning his career, O'Connell recently wrote to the authors that his "favorite role was that of Howard Bevans, both on the stage and in the film, of *Picnic*, and God rest William Inge's soul."

Reta Shaw was born in South Paris, Maine, on Friday the 13th, in the month of September, of English-Scotch-Irish descent. She attended South Paris high school, where she was an excellent student. In fact, she was awarded fifty dollars in gold upon graduation for being the best "all-round" student in the class. Her parents had encouraged her to pursue any course she wished, although her musician father did teach her to play the piano—an accomplishment that was later to be of great importance.

Miss Shaw's original ambition to become a missionary was soon overcome by the call of the stage. Being from a small town, she was extremely active in school and church functions and was soon taking part in many local plays.

After graduation from high school, the would-be actress enrolled in the Leland Powers School of the Theatre in Boston. Miss Shaw later taught dramatics at the Bishop-Lee School in Boston and Children's Theatre at the Buffalo Little Theatre.

Trying to get started in the theatre in New York was the most difficult situation Miss Shaw ever encountered. She augmented her dwindling funds

Reta Shaw in *Mary Poppins*.

series, and of Aunt Lil in the "Mr. Peepers" series. She has appeared on *The Ann Sothern Show*; *The Andy Griffith Show*; *Ichabod and Me*; *The Red Skelton Show*; *The Lucy Show*; *Bob Hope Presents*; *Bewitched*; *I Spy*; *That Girl*; and many others, and is a familiar face to millions of Americans.

Eduard Franz was born on October 31, 1902, in Milwaukee, Wisconsin, to a nontheatrical family of ten. His father was a retired sea captain. Franz enrolled in the Layton Art School in Milwaukee. The school was located across the street from The Wisconsin Players, a little theatre. Franz, who could not decide whether to be an artist or an actor, divided his time between the two. After leaving the art school he spent nine months as a commercial artist and worked with Coffer-Miller Players, a Chicago repertory company. In the mid-1920s, he went to Broadway and appeared in several plays. During the Depression, he and his wife, Margaret, farmed in Texas and Wisconsin. In the mid 1930s, he returned to New York and appeared as Shylock

by playing piano in clubs and hotels while she did one-woman shows, monologues and play readings for women's clubs, ladies' nights, and anyone who would pay to listen.

Miss Shaw's first major appearance was with the national touring company of *Annie Get Your Gun* with Mary Martin, after which she appeared in the Broadway productions of *It Takes Two, Gentlemen Prefer Blondes* with Carol Channing, *Picnic*, and *Pajama Game*.

During World War II, she spent twenty-nine months overseas as a recreational worker with the American Red Cross, serving in Iceland, England, France, Belgium, and Germany.

Working with such stage greats as Joshua Logan and George Abbott are numbered among her greatest thrills.

Since moving to the West Coast from New York, she has appeared in numerous movies including *Picnic*; *Pajama Game*; *Mary Poppins*; *Pollyanna*; *Global Affair*; *Bachelor in Paradise*; *Lady Takes a Flyer*; *That Funny Feeling*; and *The Loved One*.

Among Miss Shaw's television roles, she is probably best remembered for her portrayal of Martha, the housekeeper, in "The Ghost and Mrs. Muir"

Eduard Franz.

17

Eduard Franz and Lana Turner in _Latin Lovers._

in a modern version of _The Merchant of Venice_. He appeared in a number of good plays over the next decade. In 1947 he accepted an offer to appear in 20th Century-Fox's _The Iron Curtain_ and moved to California where he still lives. Over the past twenty-five years, Franz has appeared in countless television shows and one series, "Breaking Point," in 1964. He has also taken up his painting again. In recent years he has had a showing of his work at the Attria Gallery in Los Angeles. Mrs. Franz is a fabric designer as well. His favorite film roles include the Major in _The Iron Curtain_; Brandeis in _The Magnificent Yankees_; the Cantor in _The Jazz Singer_; the Indian in _Broken Lance_; and the Indian Chief in _White Feather_.

Franz modestly wrote, "none of them great but I enjoyed doing them."

Bill Quinn was born on May 6, 1912, in New York

City. His mother was a bit player in early silent films and a chorus singer in several Broadway productions. His father supervised the photostat department for the United States Shipping Board. Quinn worked in silent films as a child in New York beginning in 1916 or 1917. His first Broadway appearance was in David Belasco's _Daddies_ with Jeanne Eagles in 1918. He toured with several companies in the 1920s and appeared with Big Bill Tilden in two plays, _Don Quixote, Jr._ and _They All Want Something_ in 1926 and 1927. He appeared in _Gentlemen of the Press_ in 1928 and for C.B. Cunningham's _As Good as New_, starring Otto Krueger, in 1929 to 1930. During the Depression he was brought into radio in 1933 by an old friend from Broadway, Courtney Savage, at CBS. Quinn played on radio almost exclusively in New York until 1958 when he entered films and television. He did almost every radio show that originated from

New York at one time or another including: *"Mr. District Attorney;" "Gangbusters;" "Your FBI in Peace and War;" "The Shadow;" "The Mollé Mystery Theatre;"* and *"Counterspy."* He replaced Richard Widmark in *"Front Page Farrell,"* and appeared on other daytime serials such as *"John's Other Wife;" "Just Plain Bill;"* and *"When a Girl Marries."* He estimates that he performed on more than six-thousand radio broadcasts. After going to Hollywood he has appeared in a number of feature films since 1958 including: *The Last Angry Man; Ada; The Mountain Road; Advise and Consent;* and *Cry for Happy.*

For four years he was seen as "Sweeney," the bartender on television's *"The Rifleman."* Quinn has been married for thirty-three years and has three grown daughters. The eldest, Virginia, is married to comedian Bob Newhart. The middle daughter, Eileen, is a stewardess for Western Air Lines, and the youngest, Mary Ellen, is a professional singer.

Bill Quinn

Bill Quinn, second from right, with Don Knotts in *The Reluctant Astronaut*.

Miss Isabella Withers, however, is a prime example of the hardworking-professional actress who worked for many years in relative anonymity. Isabella Irene Withers was born January 20, 1896, in Frankton, Indiana, a daughter of Edward H. and Minnie Snow Withers. Her father worked in a glass factory in Frankton during the winter months. When the factory shut down for the summer, he returned to Moweaqua, Illinois, where he conducted a photo business. The family continued to reside in Frankton, spending their summers in Moweaqua, until 1903 when they moved to Coffeyville, Kansas. Isabella attended the Coffeyville schools and was graduated from high school in 1914. After graduation she attended the Georgia Brown Dramatic School in Kansas City, where advanced students could be seen by producers. Her first job was replacing an actress in a play at the O.D. Woodward Theatre in Kansas City. After dramatic school she went on the Chautauqua circuit which was very popular then.

In August of 1916 she signed with the Pagent Film Company in Kansas City. She appeared as the Sunflower Princess in a film short, filmed in Kansas City.

In May of 1917 she was playing on stage at the

Isabella Withers.

Jefferson Theatre in Coffeyville, Kansas. She had the role of Vera in *The Melting Pot*. After their engagement, the company took the production to Fort Worth, Texas. Apparently she appeared in amateur theatrical productions during her high school years at the Jefferson Theatre.

In 1919 or 1920 she was on stage in *Cappy Ricks* at the Lincoln Theatre, Decateur, Illinois. In February, 1920, she was playing somewhere in her native Indiana. From Indiana the company moved east. In May of 1920 she was playing on stage in Chicago in *Keep Her Smiling*. After their engagement the company went to California where they played two week engagements in the larger California cities.

In February, 1921, she played at Cohan's Grand Theatre in Chicago in *The Tavern*. It had a lengthy run in Chicago. Also in the cast were Lowell Sherman and Joseph Allen. The entire production was under the personal supervision of George M. Cohan. In May of 1921 the company took the production to Cleveland and Atlantic City.

During the 1920s one of her longest runs was in the play, *Rain*, which was staged at the Alcazar Theatre in San Francisco, where she received "rave" notices in *Rain*—and she took many, many curtain calls.

Miss Withers began her Hollywood film career when, in 1930, she appeared in the 1930 M-G-M film, *Paid*, opposite Joan Crawford, Robert Armstrong, Marie Prevost, Kent Douglas and Hale Hamilton. She also appeared in a two-reel comedy, *The Big Scoop*, opposite Frank McHugh. In 1932 she appeared in a two-reel Edgar Kennedy short, *Mother-In-Law's Day*.

She appeared in several other feature films in the 1930s and appeared as the Floor Nurse in the 1941 Warner Brothers-First National Picture, *Manpower*. In 1944 she appeared in Paramount's *Practically Yours*, opposite Claudette Colbert, Fred MacMurray, Gil Lamb, Cecil Kellaway, Robert Benchley, Tom Powers, Jane Frazee, and Dorothy Granger. In the same year, she appeared as the nurse that helps Casanova (Gary Cooper) in *Casanova Brown*, an RKO-Radio picture.

In 1947 she appeared a second time in a Joan Crawford feature film, *Possessed*, in the role of Nurse Rosen. In 1948 she appeared as a secretary in Warner Brothers,' *The Fountainhead*. In 1951 she appeared as Mrs. Wood opposite James Dunn, Allene Roberts and Arthur Shields in *A Wonderful*

Life, a film produced by the Congregational Christian Churches. She also became a regular member of the cast of *"The Life of Riley"* television series and did leads in pictures with Red Skelton and Jack Benny.

Miss Withers was always a very shy, modest, and self-effacing person. A thorough professional, her lot in life was the relative anonymity of a character actress.

Isabella Irene Withers passed away in Hollywood in September, 1968. Following services in California, her ashes were sent to Moweaqua, Illinois, for interment. Few people remember her career, even though her contribution to films was sizable when viewed from the perspective of acting competence. Her other film credits included: *Brother Rat; Mission to Moscow; I Love a Mystery; The Gay Senorita; To Each His Own*, and *Tonight We Sing*.

Charles Halton was an extremely versatile actor, with a deft and subtle touch for comedy, but because of his powerful delivery he became typecast as a villain throughout his lengthy film career. His widow, Mrs. Lilah C. Halton, wrote that "the irony of this gentle meticulous man with the just mind being cast as a heavy never fails to amuse me." Despite occasional deviations into some fondly remembered Milquetoast characterizations, however, he was best known for his grouchy identification as a heavy in many films.

Halton was born on March 16, 1876, in Washington, D.C. His father, an attorney in Washington, and his mother, German born, lived in a comfortable home in the now fashionable section of Georgetown. After his father's death in 1882, Charles, his mother, and two sisters went to Germany to live with the maternal grandparents for three years. When they returned to the United States they took up residence in New York City. At a very early age it became necessary for Halton to work, delivering papers. He sneaked out of the house at night on the pretext of peddling papers but also had "a chance to view in person or even exchange a word or two with those illustrious thespians of that day and age."

He quit school at fourteen, but he was naturally ascetic and therefore read assiduously. Halton's employer, upon discovering his interest in the theater, financed his enrollment in the New York Academy of Dramatic Arts. After graduating, he

Charles Halton.

joined the Lillian Russell Company and toured throughout the country.

Halton had a long career on the Broadway stage in a number of noteworthy plays. His best remembered role was perhaps that of Glougower in *Once in a Lifetime*, which was a part for which he was closely identified. He appeared in several silent and talking films from 1918 to 1935. When he closed in the New York run of Dodsworth, he went with Walter Houston to Hollywood to do the screen version. Halton remained in Hollywood the rest of his life, doing picture after picture, except for an occasional New York play.

It was in Los Angeles that he met his wife, Lilah, a widow with three partially grown children. Mrs. Halton wrote that "Mr. Halton fell in love with all of us." It was his only marriage.

Among his associates, Halton was known for his beautiful speaking voice and flawless use of the English language. However, except when playing Shakespearean roles, Halton had an uncanny ability to assume a voice suitable to the character he was playing. He played in scores of films and was

Charles Halton, right, with Sidney Toler and Sally Blane in
Charlie Chan at Treasure Island.

active in television. He died on April 16, 1959, at the age of eighty-three. According to Mrs. Halton, her husband appeared in approximately 160 films which included: *Dodsworth; The Black Legion; Dead End; Prisoner of Zenda; Young in Heart; Dr. Cyclops; Sabotage; A Tree Grows in Brooklyn; A Star is Born;* and *Friendly Persuasion.*

Grant Mitchell was a familiar figure on the American screen for nearly a quarter of a century. A short, stocky man, he was best known for his portrayals of fusty comic fathers, meek bank clerks and similar roles in which he nearly always wore pince-nez glasses.

Mitchell was born on June 17, 1874, in Columbus, Ohio, and was educated at Phillips Academy, Andover, Yale College, and Harvard Law School.

He practiced law for three years before turning to acting. After studying at the American Academy of Dramatic Arts he made his stage debut in Chicago in 1902 with Richard Mansfield in *Julius Caesar.* For the next thirty years Mitchell was consistently active as a leading man and comedian on the American stage. During his Broadway career he played leading roles in such plays as: *The Tailor-Made Man; The Whole Town's Talking; It Pays to Advertise; The Champion; The Hero;* and *The Baby Cyclone.*

Mitchell went to Hollywood in 1933 to launch a film career that included roles in more than a hundred pictures over the course of the next twenty-four years. Among his better known characterizations were those in: *Man to Man; Central Airport; Dinner at Eight; Saturday's Millions;*

The Show-Off; Golddiggers of 1935; A Midsummer Night's Dream; The Life of Emile Zola; Hollywood Hotel; It Happened on Fifth Avenue; The Man Who Came to Dinner; Arsenic and Old Lace; See Here Private Hargrove; Laura; A Medal for Benny; The Last Gangster; and films in the *Blondie* series.

A bachelor, Mitchell once said that "stage wives are the only ones I ever had." He was a resident of the old Hollywood Hotel for many years until it was torn down in 1956. He was one of the last permanent residents to leave. His home in New York was at the Yale Club. Despite his age, he successfully persuaded the United States Army to allow him to go to the South Pacific to entertain in camp shows during World War II. Mitchell made his last stage appearance in 1947, starring in *Accidentally Yours* at the Biltmore Theatre in Los Angeles.

Grant Mitchell, center, with Robert Walker and Donna Reed in *See Here, Private Hargrove*.

Grant Mitchell, center, with Rose Hobart and Humphrey Bogart in *Conflict*.

Mitchell collapsed April 19, 1956, in a Hollywood Boulevard drugstore and was hospitalized until his death May 1, 1957, at the Wilshire Sanitarium. His sizable estate was distributed not only among surviving relatives, but a portion of it was also bequeathed to his longtime business manager and friend, Don L. Greenwood. Mitchell described his friend in the will as "primarily responsible for the savings which comprise my estate" and as "particularly helpful in looking after my needs."

Several generations of moviegoers came to know Donald Meek, a slight, bald, quavering-voiced character actor as the representative of the typical average man. On the stage or screen he was usually confused, a man who was burdened down by feelings of timidity and ineffectuality. To audiences, by virtue of his name and deportment, he was truly the professional Milquetoast. The diminutive character actor played more than eight hundred roles in his stage and screen career of fifty-eight years.

Born in Glasgow, Scotland, July 14, 1880, Meek was the son of Scotch-Presbyterian Matthew Meek, an artist. When he was fourteen he came to the United States as "top man" in an acrobatic troupe, but a fall in Hamilton, Ontario, in which he broke both legs, turned him to acting. Meek was forced to become a character actor at eighteen when a bout of tropical fever contracted while he was serving in the Army in Cuba (during the Spanish-American War) caused him to lose most of his hair. Meek was turned down for service in World War I when he tried to enlist again with the American forces, and so he went to Canada to join the Princess Pats.

Donald Meek, left, with James Stewart in *Come Live with Me.*

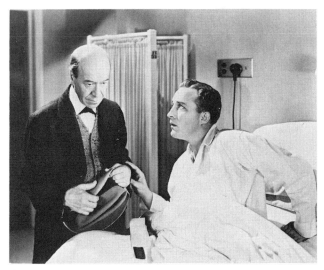

Donald Meek, left, with Bing Crosby in *Pennies from Heaven*.

As a young man he joined the Castle Square Stock Company in Boston and played with them for many years. His first New York performance was in 1913 in a musical, *Going Up*. An engagement with the Countess Stock Company in Denver, Colorado, led to his marriage to the former Belle Walken in 1909 in Boston. After World War I, he toured South Africa, India, and Australia in road shows, returning to Broadway to begin a long stand in such plays as: *Broken Dishes; Love'em and Leave'em; Six Cylinder Love; Little Old New York;* and *After Tomorrow*.

Meek's screen debut was made in 1928, but movie acting became full time only in 1933 when he came to Hollywood in a leading role in *Of Thee I Sing*. In the succeeding thirteen years he made more than one hundred films. At five feet, four inches and 130 pounds he often played the comic Milquetoast type of character and only occasionally enacted the menace. His favorite roles were the little Irishman in *The Informer* and the zany toymaker in *You Can't Take It With You*. Movie audiences recall Meek best for these and other roles in such films as: *Mrs. Wiggs of the Cabbage Patch; Captain Blood; Pennies from Heaven; Artists and Models; The Adventures of Tom Sawyer; Little Miss Broadway; Hold That Coed; Barbary Coast; Stage Coast; Keeper of the Flame; Bathing Beauty;* and *Colonel Effingham's Raid*.

On November 8, 1946, Meek was taken to the Hollywood Presbyterian Hospital where he was treated for leukemia. He had been working on his first film in more than a year, Robert Riskin's, *Magic Town*. Meek died on November 18, and because several scenes were unfinished in the picture, the script was revised so that his completed scenes remained in the picture. After the funeral the body was sent to Denver for burial.

Roscoe Ates, a rubber-faced comedian, literally stuttered his way to popularity, even though he had cured himself of stammering at the age of eighteen. Known as a "scene stealer" in all entertainment media with his "Casper Milquetoast" type of characterizations, Ates never seemed able to reach any goal he sought, on or off-stage. When he died he had earned a sizable fortune and had little left of it. He died from lung cancer at the age of sixty-seven on March 1, 1962, at the West Valley Community Hospital in Encino, California.

Ates's frustrated screen roles were reflected in real life as he progressed through a succession of well publicized marital difficulties through the years. His best-known role was that of a ranch roustabout in Western pictures, and his trademark was his pliable, mobile face, which he twisted around like a mass of putty, and his long, drawn-out stutter and pop eyes which made him a comically appealing figure to movie audiences.

Born in Grange, Mississippi, January 20, 1895, he played for fifteen years in vaudeville and repertory shows before entering the movies in 1930. While studying the violin as a student in a conservatory in Warren, Ohio, he discovered in a group singing class that he had no stutter when he sang. Ates rid himself of his speech defect by reciting song lyrics, then practicing tongue-twisting words in front of a mirror. After coming to Hollywood, Ates attracted the attention of film director Wesley Ruggles, who gave him a role in the movie *Cimarron*. He later appeared in a number of successful pictures with Marie Dressler, Wallace Beery and Polly Moran.

During World War II he spent two years as a major in the Army Air Corps. He was placed on inactive duty in 1944, but finished the war as a USO entertainer. Ates married his first wife, Clara Adrian, in 1922, and they were divorced thirteen years later. In 1938 he wed his vaudeville partner, Lenora Bell Ates, known professionally as Barbara Ray. She divorced him in 1944, but they were remarried in 1949. She died of leukemia in 1955. His

Roscoe Ates in *The People's Enemy*.

Roscoe Ates, center, with Lee Morgan and Eddie Dean in *Shadow Valley*.

last wife was the former Mrs. Beatrice Martinez, whom he married in Las Vegas in December, 1960, when he was sixty-five and she twenty-six.

Ates's many films included: *Cimarron; Alice in Wonderland; Merry Wives of Reno; Untamed; Captain Caution; Chad Hanna; Affairs of Jimmy Valentine; Palm Beach Story; Gone with the Wind; Stranger Wore A Gun; Those Redheads from Seattle; Come Next Spring; Lucy Gallant;* and *Birds and the Bees*. His last movie was *Errand Boy*, starring Jerry Lewis.

In his last years he worked infrequently in television but was confined to the hospital for six weeks in 1961, suffering from lung cancer. A relapse returned him to the hospital in February where he fought gamely against the disease but finally succumbed.

John Qualen is one of the most active and versatile character actors in the history of the American film. Since the early 1930s, he has played countless character parts including the sailors, wistful Scandinavian janitors, pitiful little men, and foreigners.

Qualen was born on December 8, 1899, in Vancouver, British Columbia, and came to this country when he was a year old. His father, a Norwegian Lutheran pastor from 1897 to 1955, changed congregations every few years and the family moved from Slayton, Minnesota, to Marshalltown, Iowa, and then to Ottawa, Aurora and Elgin, Illinois. In Elgin, Qualen won an oratorical contest and was awarded a year's scholarship to Northwestern University. He ran out of money after six months, so he shifted to the Lyceum Arts Conservatory in Chicago where he studied not only dramatics but the flute.

In 1924, he married Pearle Larson, whom he had first met in Marshalltown when he was eight years old. With his wife, Qualen played the Lyceum-Chautauqua circuit, a series of tent shows in the summer and appearances in small colleges and opera houses in winter. When sound motion pictures came in, Qualen moved on to New York. He played on many radio shows playing character parts. His first big break came when Elmer Rice was casting *Street Scene* and Qualen tried out and won his now famous role of the Swedish janitor. *Street Scene* won the Pulitzer Prize and ran for months. When Samuel Goldwyn brought *Street Scene* to the screen in 1931, he brought Qualen and several other actors of the original cast to Hollywood. John Ford saw his performance, immediately hired him to play a Swede in Sinclair Lewis' *Arrowsmith*, with Ronald Coleman and Helen Hayes.

John Qualen in *The Grapes of Wrath*.

John Qualen, right, with Elizabeth Hartman in *A Patch of Blue.*

Rice took him back to New York to play *Counselor at Law* with Paul Muni for two years. Again, several members of the New York cast were brought to Hollywood by director William Wyler and Qualen was one of them. After *Counselor at Law*, he appeared in a series of movies, including *Whipsaw*, with Myrna Loy and Spencer Tracy. It was this picture, in which Qualen played a helpless father of a sick child, that prompted Darryl Zanuck to cast him in the role of Papa Dionne in *The Country Doctor*.

Qualen has made over 170 pictures in his long career. Some of his most memorable parts include: Muley in *Grapes of Wrath*; Alex Larson in *Long Voyage Home*; and as the fisherman in *The High and the Mighty*. He has played countless Germans, Swedes, Irishmen, Canadians, Italians, and Norwegians during the past thirty-five to forty years.

Other pictures include: *His Girl Friday; The Searchers; Hans Christian Anderson; Unchained; Two Rode Together; A Patch of Blue; The Prize; The Seven Faces of Dr. Lao; A Big Hand for the Little Lady; The Man Who Shot Liberty Valance; Cheyenne Autumn; The Sons of Katie Elder;* and *Firecreek*. He has also appeared on many top-rated television shows, including *Ben Casey; Andy Griffith; The Lawman; Bonanza; Mr. Ed; My Favorite Martian;* and *The Danny Thomas Show*.

The Qualens moved to Los Angeles in 1933 and have lived in their present Westwood home since 1936. They have three daughters, Betty, Meredith, and Kathleen, and ten grandchildren. Qualen is treasurer of the Authors Club, founded in 1940 by Rupert Hughes, and is historian of the Masquers.

Frank Puglia has often been seen in such parts as a priest, waiter, or cafe owner. He was born on March 9, 1892, in Linguaglossa, Cantania, Italy, into a rather well-to-do family. The father, Salvatore, was left with the care of the five Puglia children when the mother, Annetta, died at the age of twenty-eight. Frank was the oldest child, all of them boys. Salvatore Puglia's mother, "nonna" Nedda, raised the boys, since he never remarried.

Frank Puglia was a soloist in his church choir at the age of thirteen as well as a member of a traveling operetta company. His father decided to go to the United States with the three oldest children and arrived in New York on August 14, 1907. Frank became an employee in his uncle's laundry at a salary of three dollars a week. In 1908 he answered

Frank Puglia.

an ad for an Italian theatre at Fourth and Bowery Streets, and thus began a career in what he now calls "good, bad, very bad, mediocre companies, in dramas, comedies, and operettas." He traveled all over the United States as well as in South America.

In 1915 he married his beloved Irene. In the summer of 1921 he was engaged as an all-around performer in a stock company playing at the old Olympic Theatre on East Fourteenth Street near Third Avenue in New York. He played the villainous brother in a tearjerker, *The Two Orphans*, and his performance was witnessed by D.W. Griffith. Griffith gave Puglia the part of the "good" brother in the epic film, *Orphans of the Storm*, starring Lillian and Dorothy Gish, Joseph Schildkraut and Sheldon Lewis as his brother. This was Puglia's first film and in his words the "beginning of my lucky career."

Puglia's favorite characterizations from among his many varied roles were as: Pancho Villa's father in *Viva Villa*; a villain in *Charlie Chan in Panama*; the chief of police in *Torrid Zone*; the padre in *Arise, My Love*; the cab driver in *Now*

Frank Puglia, left, with Claudette Colbert in *Without Reservations*.

Voyager; the horse jumper in *Stallion Road*, the chief of police in *Meet the Wildcat*; the opera conductor in *The Phantom of the Opera*; a cowardly traitor in *Ali Baba and the Forty Thieves*; a pundit in *Jungle Book*; Pedro, the troubador in *Billy the Kid*; Dr. Abramonte in *Yellow Jack*; the opera conductor in *May Time*; the innkeeper and opera conductor in *Balalaika*; and the Japanese diplomat in *Blood on the Sun*.

He also personally enjoyed his role as "Tony" on the live television adaptation of "*They Knew What They Wanted*." Other screen credits include: *This Is the Life*; *Roughly Speaking*; *Song to Remember*; *Together Again*; *Lost Moment*; *Road to Rio*; *Joan of Arc*; *Special Agent*; *Walk Softly Stranger*; *The Caddy*; *Shanghai*; *Serenade*; *Black Orchid*; and *Girls, Girls, Girls*.

Puglia now lives happily with his wife of more than fifty years in Los Angeles. When asked recently to comment on any reminiscences of his long film-acting career he related to the authors:

"Hopes, disillusions, tears, laughter, anguish, successes, hopes, flops, rages, hunger, illusion, beliefs, disbeliefs, stupidity (surely on my own part), stupidity (on their part, maybe), sickness, recoveries...all in all, a very lucky "nobody" who wouldn't change his troubles, past or present, his happiness, past or present, for anything in the world."

A rather beautiful statement for a man who claims to learn his English through the newspapers.*

From these short biographies and the ones to follow, it is comforting to remember that Hollywood films were once filled with vignette performances by such vastly talented supporting players—the "character people." They were often given only a few lines and a moment in the spotlight, but they made their presence felt with great acting skill and we thank them for it. We hope that this volume will help the reader bask in the unforgettable glow of their art.

*Frank Puglia died on October 25, 1975 in South Pasadena, California.

30

CHARACTER PEOPLE

Mimi Aguglia
1885-1970

Mimi Aguglia started her career on the stage in her native Italy and toured the continent doing roles in French, Spanish and English in addition to Italian. In approximately 1910, Charles Frohman brought her to Broadway and for some years thereafter she worked the two continents alternately. She also toured the capitals of South America.

Among her stage roles were *Hamlet* and one part she did everywhere—*Madame X*. Late in her career she went to Hollywood where she played character roles in films including *Cry of the City*; *The Outlaw*; *Captain from Castile*; *When in Rome*; *The Rose Tattoo*; *The Brothers Rico*; *That Midnight Kiss*; and *Black Hand*.

Ben Alexander in *Man in the Shadow*.

Mimi Aguglia, center, with J. Carrol Naish and Jose Iturbi in *That Midnight Kiss*.

Ben Alexander
1911-1969

Ben Alexander was born in Goldfield, Nevada on May 26, 1911. He was a child star and made his movie debut at the age of three when he played cupid in *Each Pearl A Tear* and continued in silent films for eleven years. He attended the University of California and Stanford but left school to become a radio announcer.

In the 1930s he became an announcer for such

shows as: "Queen For a Day;" "Father Knows Best;" "Charlie McCarthy;" "Anniversary Club;" "Brenthouse;" and "Heart's Desire." He returned to Stanford but left again when he found acting more lucrative.

He gained his greatest following as Detective Frank Smith on the "Dragnet" television show beginning in 1952. He also was seen on television later on in "Felony Squad." He was a shrewd businessman and became wealthy from various investments. He died July 5, 1969.

His films included: *All Quiet on the Western Front*; *Penrod and Sam*; *Tom Brown of Culver*; *Stage Mother*; *Annapolis Farewell*; *The Spy Ring*; *The Leather Pushers*; *Dragnet*; and *Man in the Shadow*.

John Anderson
1922-

John Anderson was born in Clayton, Illinois. He began his acting career on the Mississippi River showboat, *Goldenrod*, in 1942. He entered the service during World War II and following the war completed a masters degree in drama at the University of Iowa.

After a year with the Cleveland Playhouse, Anderson went to New York appearing in off-Broadway and Broadway productions. He played Gooper in the Broadway productions of *Cat on a Hot Tin Roof*. While touring the country in that production he was brought to the attention of Hollywood.

He has appeared in over five hundred television productions and thirty motion pictures. His heavy schedule in films and television has not kept him from his first love, the stage. His film credits include: *Psycho*; *Ride the High Country*; *Cotton Comes to Harlem*; *Soldier Blue*; *Walk on the Wild Side*; and *Geronimo*. He was also awarded the Western Heritage Award at the National Cowboy Hall of Fame in 1967.

John Anderson.

Pedro Armendariz
1912-1963

Pedro Armendariz was born May 9, 1912 in Mexico City. He received his early education in San Antonio, Texas and went on to study aeronautical engineering at California Polytechnic Institute. His acting career began on the stage in Mexico City. He entered films in 1935 and during the next nine years he made forty-two language films including John Steinbeck's *The Pearl*. He came to Hollywood in 1947 and appeared in *The Fugitive* for RKO. He appeared in over ninety films in the United States of America and often appeared with his close friend, John Wayne. While filming *From Russia with Love* he became ill with cancer and he ended his life with a self-inflicted gunshot wound on June 18, 1963.

His films included: *Three Godfathers*; *Fort Apache*; *Tulsa*; *The Conqueror*; *The Big Boodle*; *The Little Savage*; *The Wonderful Country*; *Captain Sinbad*; and *My Son, the Hero*.

Pedro Armendariz.

Edward Asner
1929-

Edward Asner, the youngest of five children, was born in Kansas City, Kansas. After graduation from their public schools, he attended the University of Chicago where he began to act on the stage of the University Theatre. His acting was interrupted from 1951 to 1953 with service in the Army Signal Corps. Stationed in France, he did not resume his career until he returned to Chicago and joined the Playwrights Theatre club, later the Drury Lane and Chevy Chase stock companies. He played leads in *Wazzek; Volpone; Threepenny Opera; The Tempest; Macbeth;* and *Goodbye My Fancy.*

Asner left Chicago and went to New York in 1955. Here he appeared in a number of off-Broadway productions, spent a season (1959) with the American Shakespeare Festival Theatre,

Stratford, Connecticut, and in 1960 the New York Shakespeare Theatre. In addition, he has appeared in numerous television productions in New York and Los Angeles, the most well-known one being "The Mary Tyler Moore Show."

His many films include: *Satan Bug; The Slender Thread; Eldorado; Change of Heart; The Venetian Affair; Peter Gunn; They Call Me Mr. Tibbs; Skin Game;* and *Don't Throw Cushions into the Ring.* His favorite role was the slave trader in *Skin Game.* Asner is married and has three children. His hobbies—gardening, reading, and enjoying his children.

Edward Asner.

Malcolm Atterbury

Born in Philadelphia, Malcolm Atterbury had an illustrious 20 year career in the theatre, playing on Broadway, in concerts, vaudeville, and musicals before going to Hollywood and films. Having played

Malcolm Atterbury.

Felix Aylmer, right, with Hayley Mills in *The Chalk Garden*.

so many diverse characterizations, he almost defies identification. He has played murderers, sheriffs, gangsters, businessmen, medicine men, politicians, and doctors.

Atterbury, the son of General W.W. Atterbury, President of the Pennsylvania Railroad for twenty-five years, was slated for a different career from the one chosen by his father. Architecture was the General's objective, but the young Atterbury rebelled.

After working in radio, summer stock, operating playhouses, a night club, and restaurant, and freelance theater work, he moved to Hollywood in 1953. His first picture was the film, *Dragnet*, followed by such roles as: *Stranger at my Door*; *Reprisal*; *No Time for Sergeants*; *Rio Bravo*; *North by Northwest*; *Summer and Smoke*; *Advise and Consent*; *The Birds*; and *Hawaii*. His television work includes such series as: "Gunsmoke;" "Dragnet;" "The Westerner;" "Perry Mason;" and "Playhouse 90."

Atterbury is an artist and an ardent Dodger fan. Both he and his wife are tournament bridge players. He also works at his stamp collection which he started as a youngster.

Felix Aylmer
1889-

Born in Corsham, England, of nonprofessional parents, educated at Oxford, Aylmer made his stage debut in 1911 in *Cook's Man*, London. The American debut came on the stage in New York in 1922 in *Loyalties*.

A nimble-minded actor whose brand of make-believe guarantees audiences their money's worth, Aylmer had had a most distinguished career on the stage and screen. His first screen role was in a German picture called *Hocus-Pocus*. Earlier films which followed were: *Tudor Rose*; *Victoria the Great*; *South Riding*; *Major Barbara*; and *Caesar and Cleopatra*.

As to personal opinions, Aylmer is quoted: "I must confess I prefer the camera to the stage. It's easier, more comfortable." "I like the American people. So direct. So simple." Aylmer labels himself "about as English as English can be, with a dash of Wales and Scotland." Married to a retired actress with a son and daughter, he resides near London.

In 1945 he portrayed the title role of *Mr. Emmanuel* in "the best part I've ever had in films." Recent pictures have included: *Quo Vadis*; *Anastasia*; *St. John*; *Separate Tables*; *Doctor's Dilemma*; *From the Terrace*; and *Exodus*.

Jim Backus
1913-

Jim Backus was born in Cleveland, Ohio. After an uneventful childhood, he was graduated from the University School and then went to New York. In New York he was graduated from the American Academy of Dramatic Arts and began a career in the theatre.

He played numerous roles in summer stock and appeared in a succession of Broadway flops. Between engagements Backus began to work in radio. At one time he did more than thirty programs a week.

After the war he went to Hollywood appearing in more than seventy-five motion pictures. Television followed with starring roles in the series: "I Married Joan;" "The Jim Backus Show;" and "Gilligan's Island."

One of the funniest people in show business, Backus's talent is in constant demand. Among his many film credits are: *Ice Palace*; *It's a Mad, Mad, Mad, Mad, Mad World*; *Bright Victory*; *Androcles and the Lion*; *I Love Melvin*; *Boys' Night Out*; *I'll See You in My Dreams*; and *Deadline U.S.A.* Perhaps his most memorable performance was the role of James Dean's father in *Rebel Without a Cause*. He has won the coveted "Oscar" twice for his creation, the nearsighted Mr. Magoo.

Art Baker
1898-1966

Art Baker gained his widest audience as the master

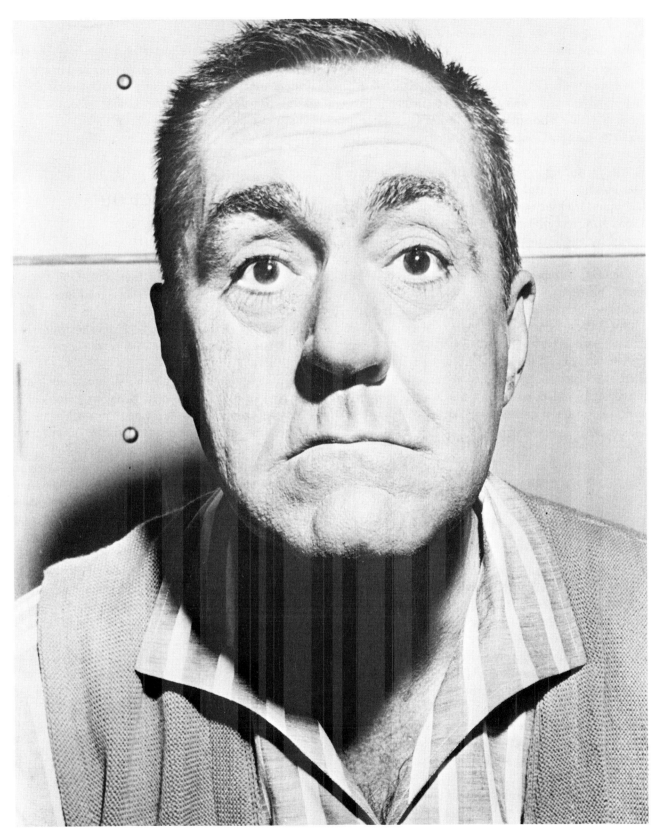

Jim Backus in *It's a Mad, Mad, Mad, Mad World*.

Art Baker in *Hot Rod*.

of ceremonies of television's "You Asked for It." He kept the viewers happy for those who wanted to see the unusual. During the heyday of the show he received fifteen hundred letters a week.

He was born Arthur Shank in New York on January 7, 1898. He served in the British Army during World War I. After the war he went into sales work and was hired by Forest Lawn to lecture on its stained glass window depicting "The Last Supper." When they advertised on the radio he became their announcer.

His first film was under his real name of Arthur Shank, *Artists and Models* in 1937. He later adopted the name Art Baker and was particularly effective as the crooked politician, "A. J. Finley," in *The Farmer's Daughter* (1947). He died in a bank of a heart attack in Los Angeles August 26, 1966.

His film credits included: *Spellbound; Abie's Irish Rose; Daisy Kenyon; State of the Union; The Walls of Jericho; Easy Living; Any Number Can Play; Night Unto Night; Impact; Hot Rod;* and *Artists and Models.*

John Banner
1910-1973

John Banner, who played the portly, good-natured Sgt. Schultz in the television comedy series, "Hogan's Heroes," was born in Vienna, Austria. After making his debut in Vienna at the Deutsches Volks theatre, he became a romantic star. As a well known actor in pre-Hitler Germany and Austria, he left Europe, came to New York as a refugee in 1939. Unable to speak English, he learned his role phonetically and appeared on Broadway in a revue, *From Vienna*.

In 1942, he enlisted in the United States Army Air Corps and posed for a recruiting poster while in the service. He went to Hollywood in 1945 where he appeared in a number of motion pictures. However, his greatest impact as an actor was as Sgt. Schultz in "Hogan's Heroes" from 1965 to 1971.

After "Hogan's Heroes" went into reruns, he was in *The Chicago Teddy Bears* for a season and did guest spots on television and in theatrical stock.

His film roles include: *The Blue Angel; The Interns; The Fallen Sparrow; The Moon Is Down; 36 Hours; The Story of Ruth; Once Upon a Honeymoon;* and *The Juggler*.

Reginald Barlow
1866-1943

Reginald Barlow was a distinguished-looking actor who lent an air of dignity to any role he played. This was probably brought about by his military training. He was a veteran of three wars, The Spanish-American, The Boer, and World War I in which he was a colonel. He was decorated by Queen Victoria for his part in the Boer War.

Barlow was born June 17, 1866 in Springfield, Massachusetts. He made his stage debut at the age of nine with a minstrel troupe, then he performed on the legitimate stage until his last appearance in 1931, *The Silent Witness*. He died July 6, 1943 in Hollywood.

John Banner, left, with James Garner and Eva Marie Saint in *36 Hours*.

Reginald Barlow, right, with LeRoy Mason, Judith Allen, and Paul Kelly in *It Happened Out West*.

His films included: *Woman from Monte Carlo*; *Horse Feathers*; *Grand Slam*; *Flying Down to Rio*; *Half a Sinner*; *Cardinal Richelieu*; *Bride of Frankenstein*; *Werewolf of London*; *O'Malley of the Mounted*; *It Happened Out West*; *The Man in the Iron Mask*; and *The Witness Vanishes*.

Donald "Red" Barry
1912-

Donald Barry was born Donald Barry de Acosta in Houston, Texas. He was educated at the Texas School of Mines and in 1936 made his screen debut

Don Barry, left, with William Edmunds in *Ringside*.

41

in *Night Waitress* for RKO Radio. Thereafter to 1939 he appeared in numerous feature pictures including *The Woman I Love; Sinners in Paradise;* and *The Crowd Roars.*

Starting in 1939 he began to appear in western films and attained wide popularity as a Republic western star. During World War II he entertained troops overseas and was voted one of the top ten money making western stars in the Motion Picture Herald Fame Polls.

Other films in which Barry has appeared are: *Remember Pearl Harbor; Seven Men from Now; I'll Cry Tomorrow; Shalako; Bandolero; Fort Utah; Untamed Heiress;* and *Twinkle in God's Eye.*

Janet Beecher, right, with Wallace Beery in *Good Old Soak.*

James Baskett
1904-1948

James Baskett will always be best remembered for his portrayal of "Uncle Remus" in the Walt Disney classic *Song of the South* in 1946. He was born in Indianapolis on February 16, 1904 and studied to be a pharmacist. While visiting in Chicago he tried out for a stage role, and received the part; he played in Chicago stock shows for several years. Baskett moved to New York and became one of the leading Negro performers; he was featured with the Lafayette players in Harlem. While visiting in California, Freeman Gosden of "Amos 'n Andy" gave him the role of Gabby Gibson, the fast-talking lawyer on the show. He died July 9, 1948 of a heart ailment.

Janet Beecher
1885-1955

Janet Beecher was born in 1885 in Jefferson City, Missouri of the same stock that produced such notables as Harriet Beecher Stowe and Henry Ward Beecher. She spent her childhood abroad and first appeared on the stage in 1904 in a walk-on during a revival of *Two Orphans.* The following

year she had her first speaking role in *Education of Mr. Pipp* in Utica, New York. She later appeared in such stage hits as: *Believe Me; Call the Doctor; A Bill of Divorcement,* and the British production of *Widow's Might* in 1931.

In 1933 she made the first of a number of Hollywood films and specialized in playing a parent and became more or less a female Lewis Stone. She continued to play in films until 1944 when she returned to Broadway for *Slightly Scandalous.* She died August 6, 1955 in Washington, Connecticut.

Her films included: *Gallant Lady; The President Vanishes; So Red the Rose; Yellow Jack; Career; The Mark of Zorro; All This and Heaven Too; Bitter Sweet; The Lady Eve; Reap the Wild Wind; Mrs Wiggs of the Cabbage Patch;* and *Good Old Soak.*

Hank Bell
1892-1950

Hank Bell was like many film actors who appeared in scores of films in the 1930s and 1940s. Few people knew his name, they only knew his face. His primary forte was western films. He started out playing a "heavy" in his early career and usually wore a standard moustache. Bell later grew a moustache that could not be matched by any other actor. He would be found as a sidekick,

James Baskett, left, with Bobby Driscoll in *Song of the South*.

Hank Bell, right, with Iris Meredith in *Spoilers of the Range*.

sheriff, ranch hand, one of a handful of townspeople, or as in the case of John Wayne's *Flame of the Barbary Coast* in 1945, just briefly seen as a cabby.

He was born Henry Branch Bell in Los Angeles January 21, 1892 and little is known about his early life. His film career began in the mid-twenties and his films included: *Soda Water Cowboy; Beyond the Rockies; Fiddlin' Buckaroo; Young Blood; Westward Ho; The Trail of the Lonesome Pine; Colorado Trail; Geronimo; Valley of the Sun; The Man from Music Mountain;* and *Spoilers of the Range*. He died of a heart attack in Hollywood, February 4, 1950.

Robert Benchley
1889-1945

Robert Benchley was born in Worchester, Massachusetts, September 15, 1889. He was graduated from Harvard University in 1911; while there he was a cartoonist and wrote articles for the school's humor magazine, the *Lampoon*. In 1916 he joined the staff of the *New York Tribune* and wrote a number of feature stories. Benchley wrote his first book entitled *Of All Things* in 1921. Benchley became managing editor of *Vanity Fair* and wrote a column "Books and Things" for the old *New York World*. From 1920 to 1929 he was dramatic editor of the old *Life* magazine and from 1929 to 1940 was drama editor of the *New Yorker*.

During his career he wrote nearly fifty film shorts for Fox, Metro, and Paramount; he collaborated on almost as many full-length films. In 1936 he received the Motion Picture Academy Award for his short *How to Sleep*.

At one time he posed as a clown during the performance of the Ringling's Circus to gather material for a story. This began an acting career which at times interfered with his writing. Many film parts followed as well as narrating several films. His last public appearance was on the "Texaco Star Theater" radio show. Benchley suffered a stroke shortly thereafter and died November 21, 1945.

His films included: *The Major and the Minor*; *Piccadilly Jim*; *Dancing Lady*; *The Gay Divorcée*; *China Seas*; *Young and Willing*; *Road to Utopia*; *See Here, Private Hargrove*; and *Song of Russia*.

Robert Benchley.

Maurice Black
1891-1938

Maurice Black was noted for his gangster roles. He was born January 14, 1891 in Whitestone, Long Island. He started his career at the age of seventeen in vaudeville. Black went to the West Coast seven years later with a road company representing the New York stage hit, *Broadway* and stayed in Los Angeles where he entered pictures. He died of pneumonia on January 18, 1938.

Some of the films in which he appeared were: *Little Caesar*; *Common Clay*; *High Pressure*; *While Paris Sleeps*; *Dancers in the Dark*; *King Murder*; *I Cover the Waterfront*; *Sixteen Fathoms Deep*; *The Californians*; *Adventure's End*; and *The Firefly*.

Madge Blake
1900-1969

Madge Blake, the short matronly actress, is probably best remembered by audiences for her role as millionaire Bruce Wayne's Aunt Harriet on the "Batman" television series.

Miss Blake did not become an actress until after she had become a grandmother. The long delay was due to her father. Her father, a Methodist circuit rider in Kansas, discouraged her early acting ambitions. Her first film role was that of the late Spencer Tracy's mother in *Adam's Rib*. She also appeared in: *An American in Paris*; *Singing in the Rain*; *The Solid Gold Cadillac*; and *Rhapsody*. Miss Blake's television appearances in addition to "Batman" included: "Life with Father;" "Leave it to Beaver;" the old "Joey Bishop Show;" and "The Real McCoys."

Ward Bond
1903-1960

Although he was known to millions as Major Seth

Maurice Black, right, with Edward G. Robinson in *Little Caesar*.

Madge Blake, second from right, with Barbara Bates and John Ericson in *Rhapsody*.

Ward Bond.

lywood. Bond was active in industry matters and helped to found the Motion Picture Alliance. On November 5, 1960 he was to make a personal appearance during halftime at the Cotton Bowl in Dallas when he died of a heart attack in his motel room.

His pictures included: *Gone with the Wind; The Grapes of Wrath; Tobacco Road; Gentleman Jim; A Guy Named Joe; Tall in the Saddle; My Darling Clementine; Fort Apache; Three Godfathers; Operation Pacific; The Quiet Man; Mr. Roberts; Wings of the Eagle;* and *Rio Bravo.*

Hobart Bosworth
1867-1943

Hobart van Zandt Bosworth was born on August 11, 1867 in Marietta, Ohio. He was a descendant of Miles Standish. His first acting experience was in 1885 with the Rankin Stock Company in San Fran-

Adams of the popular "Wagon Train" on television, Ward Bond had a long and distinguished film career.

He was born April 9, 1903 in Bendelman, Nebraska. After high school he received a football scholarship to the University of Southern California as a tackle. Bond received his engineering degree in 1931. He and other members of the football team including John Wayne were picked by John Ford as extras for the film *Salute* in 1928. The three became lifelong friends.

After graduation he was signed by Columbia and he played small roles. Bond became a "heavy" in "B" westerns menacing such heroes as Buck Jones and Tim McCoy and also played many hoodlums and tough guy bit roles. He started getting bigger roles in 1939, particularly in films directed by John Ford.

In 1950 he starred in *Wagon Master* for Ford which was the forerunner to his role in 1957 as gruff Major Adams in "Wagon Train." He was an outspoken advocate of anti-Communism in Hol-

Hobart Bosworth.

cisco. His first New York stage appearance was with Augustin Daly's stock unit and in a short time he became known as one of the better dramatic players and romantic leading men. Bosworth played the lead in *The Sultan's Power* in 1909 which was the first film made in Los Angeles. He continued a long career in the silent films in such classics as: *The Big Parade; Monte Cristo;* and *Oliver Twist*.

In addition to his acting chores he also became a director, producer, and writer, organized his own production unit, the Bosworth Company. The company specialized in Jack London films. He continued in films until 1942 and reportedly appeared in over six hundred productions. At the time of his death on December 30, 1943 he was considered the dean of film actors.

His other films included: *The Miracle Man; Abraham Lincoln; The Hurricane; Mammy; County Fair; Last of the Mohicans; Music in the Air; The Crusades; Steamboat 'Round the Bend; Wolves of the Sea; One Foot in Heaven;* and *Sin Town*.

Pat Brady
1914-1972

Pat Brady, musician, singer, and comic sidekick of Roy Rogers, was born in Toledo, Ohio. Both parents were in show business, and Brady made his theatrical debut at the age of four in a stage production of *Mrs. Wiggs of the Cabbage Patch*.

While in high school Brady moved to California and began playing bass guitar with his father in a

Pat Brady, left, with Roy Rogers in *Down Dakota Way*.

nightclub. He was spotted by Leonard Sly, who became famous under the name Roy Rogers, who at that time was with the "Sons of the Pioneers" singing group. When he went into movies he helped Brady join the group as his replacement.

Brady stayed with the group until 1942, when he entered the United States Army. A tour of France with Patton's Third Army won him citations for valor and two Purple Hearts.

He returned to the "Sons of the Pioneers" in 1945 and left again in 1955. Brady appeared in nearly eighty motion pictures, usually as a genial Western character that he made popular. He made his jeep "Nellie Bell" a household word. Among his film credits are: *Two-Fisted Rangers*; *The Man from Music Mountain*; *Bells of Coronado*; *South of Caliente*; *The Gay Ranchero*; *The Golden Stallion*; *Down Dakota Way*; and *The Durango Kid*.

Egon Brecher
1880-1946

Egon Brecher was born February 16, 1880 in Czechoslovakia. He was a graduate of the University of Heidelberg in 1900. Brecher began his stage career in 1903 by appearing in *Sappho* on the Vienna stage. He played with touring companies in Germany and Austria and became chief director of the Stadts theatre in Vienna. Brecher migrated to the United States in 1921 and in the same year appeared on Broadway in *Liliom* opposite Eva Le Galliene. For the next dozen years he was prominent in many stage productions.

He left the stage for Hollywood in 1933 and appeared in: *To the Last Man*; *The Black Cat*; *Black*

Egon Brecher, second from left, with Effie Ellsler and Paul Muni in *Black Fury*.

49

Bob Burns, right, with Virginia Brissac in *Hill Billy Deacon*.

Fury; Charlie Chan's Secret; Sins of Man; Alibi for Murder; Black Legion; Heidi; Spawn of the North; and Four Sons. He died of a heart attack in Hollywood on August 12, 1946.

Bob Burns
1890-1956

Bob Burns is definitely the only actor to make it big by taking two gas pipes and a whiskey funnel and making it into a musical instrument. It was called a "bazooka" and this plus an ability to tell tall tales of Arkansas country folk made him one of the country's favorite comics. The name "bazooka" later was given to a weapon during World War II.

He was born in Van Buren, Arkansas on August 2, 1890 and attended the University of Arkansas. He made a fortune as a hillbilly even though he was well educated. Burns once said that he was the only person he'd ever heard of that made fifteen hundred dollars one year and four hundred thousand dollars three years later. He made his first appearance in films for Biograph in 1913 as a three dollar a day extra and didn't get the urge to play in films again until 1931. He made his first public appearance playing a mandolin in Van Buren. After inventing the "bazooka" he barnstormed for several years with a traveling carnival,

50

a sideshow in Atlantic City, and in vaudeville in a blackface act.

In 1932 he broke into radio with Rudy Vallee and Bing Crosby. He was later signed by Paramount. His films included: *If I Had A Million; Big Broadcast of 1937; Waikiki Wedding; Mountain Music; Wells Fargo; Arkansas Traveler; I'm from Missouri; Our Leading Citizen;* and *Alias the Deacon.* He invested his earnings wisely in San Fernando Valley real estate and died a wealthy man, February 2, 1956 of cancer.

Arthur Byron
1872-1943

Until his death Arthur Byron reputedly was more steadily employed on the stage or screen during his fifty-four year career than any actor before him.

He was born in Brooklyn, April 3, 1872, in a show-business family. When he was seventeen he made his first appearance in his father's company as an Indian brave. He made his New York debut one year later in *The Plunger.* During his distinguished stage career he supported the great stars of the day including Maude Adams, Ethel Barrymore, Mrs. Fiske, Katharine Cornell, and John Gielgud. While on the stage he portrayed three hundred different characters and gave ten thousand performances.

He entered films in 1932 and appeared in: *The Big Shot; 20,000 Years in Sing Sing; Mayor of Hell; Fog over Frisco; Notorious Sophie Lang; Marie Galante; The President Vanishes; The Whole Town's Talking; Oil for the Lamps of China;* and *The Prisoner of Shark Island.*

He was one of the founders of Actors Equity Association and in 1938 during turbulent times for that organization, was elected president. Byron died of a heart ailment July 17, 1943.

Frank Cady
1915-

Born in Susanville, California, Frank Cady's

Arthur Byron.

first stage appearance happened when he sang and acted in a grammar school production. During high school he appeared in a few plays, but his great interest was in writing for his hometown newspaper. He attended college and in 1938 graduated from Stanford University with a B.A. in Speech and Drama.

In 1938 he went to London where, for one year, at the Westminister Theatre, he played small parts. Cady worked in summer stock in New England and in late 1939 he returned to Stanford for two years of graduate work. From 1943 to 1946 he served in the United States Army Air Force and was stationed in England, France, and Germany. Upon his return to the United States and Hollywood he was seen by an agent in a play and signed for films.

With the impact of television upon motion pictures, Cady turned to television as parts opened up. He appeared on "Ozzie and Harriet," which led to his best-known portrayal, that of Sam Drucker, country storekeeper on "Green Acres" and "Petticoat Junction."

Frank Cady.

Film roles that he likes to remember include: *The Big Carnival; Rear Window; Flamingo Road; The Bad Seed; The Indian Fighter;* and *The Seven Faces of Dr. Lao.*

Hobbies include golf and music. Cady celebrated his thirty-second anniversary recently. He has two children and one grandchild.

Don Castle
1917-1966

Don Castle was born in Beaumont, Texas, September 29, 1917. He attended the University of Texas and sold insurance for his father. He arrived in Hollywood on a two week vacation, managed a screen test and was signed by M-G-M. His first role was as a juvenile in *Love Finds Andy Hardy* in 1938. He was being groomed for stardom when World

War II intervened and he served in the United States Army from 1942 to 1945. Upon his return he appeared in many films, but only in secondary roles or the lead in a "B" film.

He left pictures to become owner and operator of the Red Barn in Palm Springs. He later became president of Jack Wrather's International Television Corporation and for three years was associate producer of the "Lassie" television series. He never fully recovered from an automobile accident and was found dead in his Hollywood apartment on May 26, 1966 of an overdose of an unknown medication.

His films included: *Those Glamour Girls; Power Dive; World Premiere; The Searching Wind; Born to Speed; High Tide; Roses Are Red; Perilous Waters; Strike It Rich;* and *Stampede.*

Don Castle in *Stampede*.

Joseph Cawthorn
1868-1949

Joseph Cawthorn was best known in films for his marvelous German dialect which he developed on the United States stage. He was born in New York City, March 29, 1868. His first appearance on the stage was when he was only four years old, the play was a juvenile farce called *Pickaninny Minstrels.* At the age of nine he went to England and appeared in music halls for four years. He returned to the United States and performed in vaudeville and the

Joseph Cawthorn, center, with Beryl Mercer and Randolph Scott in *Broken Dreams*.

legitimate stage concentrating on musical comedies such as *Little Nugget*; *The Singing Girl*; and *Mother Goose*.

He came to Hollywood in 1926 and appeared in such films as: *Taming of the Shrew*; *Whistling in the Dark*; *Cat and the Fiddle*; *Lazy River*; *Gold Diggers of 1935*; *Naughty Marietta*; *Harmony Lane*; *The Great Ziegfeld*; *Lillian Russell*; *So Ends the Night*; *Broken Dreams*; and *The Postman Didn't Ring*.

Prior to entering films he was the favorite comedian of President Woodrow Wilson. He died of a stroke at his home in Beverly Hills January 21, 1949. His widow was actress Queenie Vassar.

Lane Chandler
1899-1972

Born in Walsh County, North Dakota, Lane Chandler has played many diversified roles on the stage, television and several hundred films.

Chandler began his career in silent movies in 1927 playing scene bits. Paramount then signed him to a term contract where he played leading roles with Betty Bronson, Esther Ralston, and Clara Bow. His favorite roles were those done for C.B. DeMille—the conductor of the train to end of

Lane Chandler, right, with Billy Vincent and Kirk Douglas in *The Big Trees*.

track in *Union Pacific* and a pirate who was a United States Navy deserter in *The Buccaneer*. His many pictures include: *Follow the Boys; The Big Trees; Saratoga Trunk; Cassanova Brown; Laura; Prince of Players; Tall Man Riding; The Spider; Great Mike;* and *Samson and Delilah*. He died September 14, 1972.

Mady Christians
1900-1951

Mady Christians was born January 19, 1900 in Vienna, Austria. It was only natural that she pursue an acting career as her father, Rudolph Christians was an actor-manager and her mother Bertha

Mady Christians, right, with Ginger Rogers in *Tender Comrade*.

Klein was an opera and concert singer. On the stage she is probably best remembered for her portrayal of Mama in *I Remember Mama* which ran on Broadway for two years. She also starred in: *Watch on the Rhine; Hamlet;* and *The Lady Who Came to Stay.* Her last Broadway role was in *The Father.*

Her films included: *A Wicked Woman; Escapade; Come and Get It; Seventh Heaven; The Woman I Love; Heidi; Tender Comrade;* and *All My Sons.* She also appeared in many European films. She died October 28, 1951.

Virginia Christine

To her many fans, Miss Christine is the charming "Mrs. Olson" on the television coffee commercials. However, the actress was born in Iowa and went to Hollywood as an accomplished pianist.

Her career has been quite successful as she be-came a busy actress appearing in over four hundred motion pictures and television productions. She made her film debut in *Edge of Darkness* with Errol Flynn. Among other top productions have been: *Mission to Moscow; Counter Attack; The Killers; High Noon; Judgement at Nuremberg; The Prize;* and *Rage to Live.*

In 1940 she married Fritz Feld, leading character actor of stage and screen. They have two grown sons, Steven and Danny. Hobbies include reading, her music, and travel. One of her favorite projects is her organizational work in Planned Parenthood of America.

William Collier Sr.

Virginia Christine.

William Collier Sr.
1866-1944

William Collier was born November 12, 1866 in New York City. He started in show business as a member of Haverly's Junior Pinafore Company. He received Shakespearean training and starred in a musical in London that he authored. From 1900 to 1920 under the Frohman management he starred on Broadway and was known as the fastest comic on stage. Collier starred in *Caught in the Rain; Never Say Die;* and *The Dictator* among many others. He was a prolific gag writer and if the script didn't suit him, Collier merely changed it to his own benefit. He teamed with George M. Cohan in many benefit performances; their hoofing and gags were always the highlight.

He went to Hollywood in 1929 and his films included: *Up the River; Six Cylinder Love; All of Me; Annapolis Farewell; Valiant Is the Word for Carrie; Josette; I'm from Missouri;* and *The Hard-Boiled Canary.*

He died January 13, 1944 leaving a son, Buster, to carry on in films.

Russell Collins
1897-1965

Russell Collins was a busy performer throughout his professional career appearing in plays, films, and television productions.

After studying drama at Carnegie Tech in Pittsburgh, Collins joined the Cleveland Playhouse in 1922. In 1932 he made his Broadway debut in *Success Story.* In later years he appeared in more than forty Broadway productions, including *The Iceman Cometh; Carousel; The Moon Is Down;* and *Calculated Risk.*

A natural for character roles, Collins became active in films and television productions. His films included: *Shockproof; Raintree County; Bad Day at Black Rock; Niagara; Soldier of Fortune;* and *The Enemy Below.* He won critical acclaim for his work in the role of the atheist in "The Chess Game," an original teleplay in 1953.

William Conrad
1920-

Born in Louisville, Kentucky, and raised in

Russell Collins.

southern California, Conrad was graduated from Excelsior High School in Bellflower, California, and then attended Fullerton Junior College where he majored in literature and drama. Upon graduation from junior college, he took a job at radio station KMPC in Beverly Hills.

In 1942 he enlisted in the Army Air Corps and earned his wings a year later. Returning to civilian life, he pursued an active career as a radio actor, starring in more than five thousand shows over the next decade.

When dramatic radio died, Conrad shifted his acting to films and also began directing.

He has appeared in several films including a memorable role as a gunman in *The Killers.* Conrad is currently starring in "Cannon" on CBS television.

When not acting, he enjoys many varied pastimes; sailplaning, hunting, and still photography. Conrad is married to former New York high-fashion model, Susan Randall. The couple has one son, Christopher, sixteen.

Conrad's film appearances have included:

William Conrad.

Sorry, Wrong Number; Cry Danger; The Ride Back; The Racket; and *Johnny Concho;* he also produced and directed *My Blood Runs Cold* and *Brainstorm.*

Philip Coolidge
1909-1967

Philip Coolidge was a veteran character actor of Broadway, movies, and television. Before going to Hollywood he appeared in such Broadway plays as *Our Town; Darkness at Noon; The Crucible;* and *Hamlet,* the latter with Richard Burton.

Coolidge divided his time between the stage and screen and was a regular on the television series, "The Farmer's Daughter."

A talented and versatile actor, Coolidge played a variety of roles in such films as *I Want to Live; The Mating Game; It Happened to Jane; North by Northwest; The Tingler; The Russians Are Coming;* and *Never a Dull Moment.*

Philip Coolidge, second from right, with Gage Clarke, Susan Hayward, and Lou Klugman in *I Want to Live*.

Ernest Cossart
1876-1951

Ernest Cossart was born on September 24, 1876 in Cheltenham, England. After he finished school he worked as a clerk for a merchant until the business folded. He then tried the stage and made his debut in April of 1896 as a gendarme in *Robert Macaire* at the old Novelty Theatre in London. Cossart had small parts in plays for several years, then his chance came for bigger roles starting with *The Duchess of Dantzig*.

In 1906 he came to New York and made his stage debut as Colonel Finkhausen in *The Girls of Göttenberg* at the old Knickerbocker Theatre. He was seen in many Theatre Guild productions and while appearing in *Mary of Scotland* in 1935 he came to Hollywood to appear in his first film, *The Scoundrel*. He died in New York on January 1, 1951.

His other films included: *The Great Ziegfeld*; *Three Smart Girls*; *The Magnificent Fraud*; *Tower of London*; *Kitty Foyle*; *Charlie's Aunt*; *King's Row*; *The Jolson Story*; and *John Loves Mary*.

Ernest Cossart, second from left, with Jennifer Jones, Sara Allgood, and Queenie Leonard in *Cluny Brown*.

Laird Cregar
1916-1944

Laird Cregar was born July 28, 1916 in Philadelphia. He was educated in England and got the acting bug playing with the Stratford-on-Avon Players. In 1936 he received a scholarship at the Pasadena Playhouse Theatre. In 1940 he was given the lead in the legitimate production of *Oscar Wilde*. His performance led to a contract with 20th Century-Fox. His six-feet-four-inch three-hundred-plus frame was just right for the villainous portrayals. His career was cut short by two heart attacks after he had gone from three hundred to two hundred pounds and he died following an operation on December 9, 1944.

His first film was *Hudson's Bay* and he also appeared in *Blood and Sand; Charley's Aunt; This Gun For Hire; Ten Gentlemen from West Point; Hello, Frisco Hello; The Lodger;* and *Hangover Square*.

Hume Cronyn in *Sunrise at Campobello*.

Laird Cregar in *I Wake Up Screaming*.

Hume Cronyn
1911-

Hume Cronyn, born in London, Ontario, Canada, is not only a distinguished character actor, but also a director and a writer.

A graduate of Ridley College, he began his acting under the auspices of the New York School of the Theatre in 1931. Cronyn's professional debut was made in Washington, D.C. with Cochran's Stock Co. in *Up Pops the Devil* in 1931. Numerous legitimate stage performances followed later as both actor and director.

Cronyn made his film debut as Herbie Hawkins in *Shadow of Doubt* at Universal in 1943. Other films have included: *The Seventh Cross; Lifeboat; The Green Years; People Will Talk; Sunrise at Campobello; Cleopatra; Gaily, Gaily; The Arrangement;* and *There Was a Crooked Man*. In addition to films, Mr. Cronyn has appeared in a number of television productions, beginning as early as 1939 for NBC.

Among his many awards was an Oscar nomination for his performance in *The Seventh Cross*. He later was nominated for an Emmy award for his work in television. In 1942 he married the actress Jessica Tandy and they have appeared together in numerous productions. They have three children. His hobby is developing his island in the Bahamas which was purchased in 1946.

She tried the legitimate stage **and was on radio for** awhile. When she finally made her way into motion pictures she had to settle for character roles (due to her age).

She appeared in many films including: *Paramount on Parade*; *If I Had A Million*; *We Live Again*; *Mr. Deeds Goes to Town*; *Artists and Models*; *The Awful Truth*; *Lillian Russell*; *Kitty Foyle*; *Blossoms in the Dust*; *Back Street*; *Cairo*; and *Above Suspicion*. She died April 17, 1959.

Cass Daley in *Crazy House*.

Cecil Cunningham
1888-1959

Cecil Cunningham could do more with a look than most actresses could do with an armful of expertise dialogue. She learned her tricks of the trade in vaudeville and later progressed into musical comedy singing and dancing in *Barber of Seville*; *Kid Boots*; *Rosalie*; and *The Pink Lady*.

Cecil Cunningham.

Cass Daley
1919-1975

Cass Daley was noted in films for her buckteeth and the ability to get her body in all sorts of shapes particularly with her rear end sticking out. When she started her film career there was no one else quite like her and this enhanced her chances of film popularity, at least for awhile.

She was born June 17, 1915 in Philadelphia.

After a short career as a hatcheck girl she soon became a performer in nightclubs. She had a brief stay with Ozzie Nelson's band as a vocalist. She then went into vaudeville until she landed her first film role in 1942 in *The Fleet's In*. More film roles followed and she also appeared as a radio performer on "Maxwell House Coffee Time" and "The Fitch Bandwagon." She retired from the screen in 1954 until she appeared in *The Spirit Is Willing* in 1967.

Other film roles include: *Star Spangled Rhythm; Crazy House; Riding High; Duffy's Tavern; Out of This World; Ladies Man; Variety Girl; Here Comes the Groom; Red Garters;* and *Norwood*. She died tragically on March 22, 1975 when she accidentally fell and embedded a piece of glass in her neck.

Steven (Steve) Darrell.

Steve Darrell
1904-1970

From 1945 through 1957 Steve Darrell appeared in many western films. He was often seen menacing Buster Crabbe, Johnny Mack Brown, Gene Autry, or Allan "Rocky" Lane.

He was born J. Steven Darrell, November 19, 1904 in Osage, Iowa, the son of a railroader. He first got the acting bug when he appeared as Abe Lincoln in grade school. Darrell moved to the West Coast in 1937 where he appeared in several plays at the Pasadena Playhouse before entering films. His first picture was a bit part in Warner's *Angels with Dirty Faces* in 1938 followed by many roles in movies and television. His favorite role was in an episode of "26 Men" on television called "Idol in the Dust." He played "Ben Salem" an ex-lawman down on his luck who joins the bad guys, but due to a friendship with a small boy, he has a change of heart and ends up the hero. He also liked a similar role in the 1955 film, *The Treasure of Ruby Hills*. He enjoyed his career as a movie player but always added that he should have become a bricklayer. He died August 14, 1970 of a brain tumor.

His films included: *Code of the Secret Service; Terrors on Horseback; Roll on Harvest Moon; Under Colorado Skies; West of Sonora; Riders in the Sky; Abandoned; Cowtown; Pecos River; The Tall Men;* and *Joe Dakota*.

Boyd Davis
1885-1963

Boyd Davis was born June 19, 1885 in Santa Rosa, California. He made his professional debut in 1907 and spent several seasons with stock and touring companies throughout the United States. His first London appearance was in 1912 in *Captain Brassbound's Conversion*. He served in World War I and when the war was over he returned to the legitimate stage in London. He returned to America and appeared in many plays on Broadway and a few silents in the 1920s. His Broadway appearances were continued through the thirties; Davis returned to films in 1941. He died in his sleep in Hollywood January 25, 1963.

Some of his films were: *You'll Never Get Rich; Harvard; Here I Come; The Ghost Ship; Colonel Effingham's Raid; Terror by Night; A Foreign Af-*

Boyd Davis, left, with Walter Pidgeon and Greer Garson in *The Secret Heart*.

fair; The Secret Heart; Ma and Pa Kettle; Samson and Delilah; Girls' School; and *At Sword's Point.*

Richard Deacon
1922-

Richard Deacon was born in Philadelphia, Pennsylvania, into a non-show business family. His father was an executive for an industrial maintenance concern.

Deacon's acting experience started at Ithaca College. Later he was actor in residence at Bennington College, Vermont, and the Barn Theatre,

Porterville, California. On Broadway, he was co-star with Phyllis Diller in *Hello Dolly*.

Best known for his comic character roles in films and television which always enliven a production, Deacon has appeared in over fifty films and innumerable television shows including the series "Leave It to Beaver," "Dick Van Dyke," and "Mothers-In-Law." His film credits list: *The Power and the Prize; Blackbeard's Ghost; The Remarkable Mr. Pennypacker; John Goldfarb, Please Come Home; Billie; That Darn Cat; Desirée;* and *The Young Philadelphians*. Favorite roles include performances in *Good Morning, Miss Dove;* and *The Solid Gold Cadillac*.

Single, Deacon has as his hobbies, rock collecting (an extensive collection), and collecting divergent painting and sculpture.

Vernon Dent
1895-1963

Richard Deacon.

"Short Subjects" were very popular in the 1920s, 1930s, and early 1940s and almost without exception they were shown before the main feature. Vernon Dent was one of the legion of players who made his living appearing in these films. It was probably a tossup whether he or Bud Jamison appeared in the most.

He was born February 16, 1895 in San Jose, California. His film career started with Mack Sennett; he appeared in Mermaid and educational comedies. He appeared with The Three Stooges; Charley Chase; Harry Langdon; Andy Clyde; and Buster Keaton in their movie shorts. Dent also was a screen writer for a few years in the thirties. He died November 5, 1963 in Hollywood.

Dent also played character parts in many features including: *Texas Cylcone*; *Million Dollar*

Vernon Dent, right, with **Lon Chaney Jr.** in *San Antonio Rose*.

Legs; The Shadow; Beasts of Berlin; Mr. Smith Goes to Washington; House of Errors; Renegades; It's Great to be Young; Cowboy Blues; And Baby Makes Three; and *Bonanza Town.*

John Dierkes
1908-1975

John Dierkes was a tall, grizzled character actor perhaps best known for his portrayal of "Morgan" in the classic western, *Shane*. He was equally at home as the robust Tennessean, "Jocko Robertson," in *The Alamo*.

He was born February 10, 1908 in Cincinnati, Ohio and was an economics major at Brown University and the University of Chicago. While working for the Treasury Department in 1946 he was assigned as a technical advisor to Columbia's *To the Ends of the Earth*. This led to a role in his first film. Prior to entering films he also worked as a copywriter, a polling service and the American Red Cross.

His pictures include: *Red Badge of Courage; Naked Jungle; The Raid; Jubal; Blood Arrow; The Hanging Tree; One-Eyed Jacks; The Comancheros;* and *The Haunted Palace.* He died January 8, 1975.

John Dierkes, left, with Emile Meyer and Jack Palance in *Shane*.

Dudley Digges, second from left, with Madeleine Carroll,
J. M. Kerrigan, and Gary Cooper in *The General Died at Dawn*.

Dudley Digges
1879-1947

Dudley Digges was one of the most respected character actors on the screen during his long film career. His stage career was even more impressive as he appeared on the New York stage for over forty years giving more than thirty-five hundred performances for the Theatre Guild alone. He was born in Dublin in 1879 and was a member of the original Abbey Players there. In 1904 he appeared with Mrs. Fiske in his New York debut. Digges was also George Arliss's right hand man for seven years assisting in many stage productions. From 1919 on he appeared in many successful plays and staged at least four. He died of a stroke on October 24, 1947 in New York.

His films included: *The Hatchet Man; Massacre; Caravan; China Seas; Mutiny on the Bounty; The General Died at Dawn; Valiant Is the Word for Carrie; The Light That Failed; Raffles;* and *The Searching Wind.*

John Dilson
1891-1944

John Dilson was born February 18, 1891 in Brooklyn. He started his career on the stage in 1909 on Broadway and had his own companies in Albany and Syracuse. He went to Hollywood in 1932 and found steady employment as a character actor playing lawyers, clerks and businessmen. Dilson died in Ventura, California June 1, 1944 leaving a brother, Clyde, to carry on the acting tradition.

His films included: *The Westerner; Hitch Hike to Heaven; Escape by Night; Women in Prison; The Man with Nine Lives; Andy Hardy's Private Secretary; Father Steps Out; Cyclone on Horseback; Pittsburgh; Mission to Moscow; Drums of Fu Manchu; Dance with the Devil* (retitled *Johnny Apollo*).

John Dilson, left, with Edward Arnold in *Johnny Apollo*.

Jimmie Dodd
1913-1964

Jimmie Dodd is best remembered as the leader and the emcee of Walt Disney's popular "Mickey Mouse Club" on television, but he was a man of many talents. He was born in Cincinnati, Ohio in 1913.

During World War II he and his wife toured overseas for the USO. Upon his return home his musical talents enabled him to win an Arthur Godfrey talent contest. Walt Disney was impressed and signed him for four years to lead the Mousketeers. His film career included assignments in the "Snuffy Smith" film series and he played "Lullaby" in the last six "3 Mesquiters" cowboy films with Tom Tyler and Bob Steele from 1942 to 1943.

During his career he composed more than four hundred songs including "Rosemary;" "Nashville Blues;" "Amarillo;" "Ginny;" and "Meet Me in Monterey." During the last year of his life he moved to Honolulu where he was scheduled to star in the new "Jimmie Dodd Aloha Show" when he succumbed to a heart attack November 10, 1964.

His films included: *Hillbilly Blitzkrieg; Valley of Hunted Men; Thundering Trails; Riders of the Rio Grande; Moon over Las Vegas; Buck Privates Come Home; Song of My Heart; Al Jennnings of Oklahoma; The Winning Team;* and *Prairie Buckaroos.*

George Dolenz
1908-1963

George Dolenz was a suave, handsome Italian who started out in life as an olive picker and tinsmith. He was born January 5, 1908 in Trieste, Italy. Prior to coming to the United States he was in the restaurant business on the Riviera. He also operated a night club in Mexico City and appeared in stock in Havana.

While attempting to further his acting interests he studied at Max Reinhardt's dramatic school in Hollywood. Dolenz supplemented his income as a waiter at the Trocadero and later became the assistant manager at Ciro's. Although he was a restaurateur, he was in demand in films. His first appearance was in the film *Unexpected Uncle* in 1941. He later signed a contract with RKO Radio Pictures, Inc. and appeared in Howard Hughes' *Vendetta* in 1950. In 1955 he became a co-owner of the Marquis, an eating establishment in Hollywood and also signed a contract to play the lead in "The Count of Monte Cristo" on television. He died February 8, 1963 at his place of business and was

Jimmie Dodd, left, with Vivian Austin in *Twilight on the Prairie*.

George Dolenz, left, with Donald Buka in *Vendetta*.

survived by his son, Mickey, who played the title role in the "Circus Boy" series.

His films included: *Moonlight in Vermont; Enter Arsene Lupin; My Cousin Rachel; Scared Stiff; Thunder Bay; A Bullet for Joey; The Purple Mask; Timbuktu;* and *The Four Horsemen of the Apocalypse.*

Ann Doran
1911-

Ann Doran was born in Amarillo, Texas, her father, Captain John R. Doran, in the Army engineers; her mother, Rose Allen, an actress. She made her first appearance on the screen in *Robin Hood* with Douglas Fairbanks in 1922, as the page to the king (Wallace Beery). Working sporadically as a child, she left the business when her family moved to San Bernadino, California, where she graduated from high school.

Miss Doran attended University of Southern California and University of California at Los Angeles returning to pictures following the death of her father in 1932. She was signed by Columbia Pictures in 1936 doing two reel comedies with Charlie Chase, Three Stooges, Andy Clyde, and various other comedians. While there, she had roles in all Frank Capra productions except *Lost Horizon.* After three years she freelanced and then signed with Paramount. On loan during this period Miss Doran made a number of pictures at Warner Brothers.

Television began about the time she left Paramount and she appeared in practically every show, finally signing with MGM's series, *National*

↓ DAN DUREYEA, NOT PAUL KELLY

Ann Doran, right, with Paul Kelly in *Fear in the Night*.

68

Don Douglas, left, with Constance Moore in *Show Business*.

Velvet. Miss Doran is still working in motion pictures and television. Among her many films are: *Rebel without a Cause; You Can't Take It with You; Mr. Smith Goes to Washington; Meet John Doe; Penny Serenade; Dive Bomber; The High and the Mighty; Fear in the Night;* and *Jackpot*.

Don Douglas
1905-1945

Don Douglas was born Douglas Kinleyside Au-

gust 24, 1905 in London, England. When he was still very young his family moved to the United States. He received his education at the New York Military Academy. At the tender age of fourteen he sang in the chorus of the Metropolitan Opera Company. He was a singer and dancer in vaudeville and appeared in New York stage musicals such as: *Desert Song; Follow Through; Rio Rita; Love Song; Nancy's Private Affair; Social Outlaw;* and *Boy Meets Girl*.

He began a busy film career in 1937 when he appeared in *Headin' East* and he was featured in seventy films the next eight years including: *Alexander's Ragtime Band; Calling Philo Vance; Charlie Chan in Panama; Show Business; Cheers for Miss Bishop; A Shot in the Dark; Little Tokyo;*

U.S.A; Tales of Manhattan; The More the Merrier; Behind the Rising Sun; Tall in the Saddle; Tokyo Rose; and *Tarzan and the Amazons.* He died December 31, 1945 following an emergency appendectomy.

Louise Dresser
1880-1965

Louise Dresser gained her greatest fame as a co-star with Will Rogers in seven films as his understanding wife. She was born Louise Josephine Karlin on October 5, 1880 in Evansville, Indiana.

She had a natural talent for acting and made her debut at the age of seventeen in amateur theatricals in Columbus, Ohio. Songwriter Paul Dresser in trying to land a job for her on the stage introduced her as his sister Louise and she took the name of Louise Dresser. She became a celebrated beauty and became a star of vaudeville, legitimate theatre, and the screen.

She introduced Paul Dresser's smash tune "My Gal Sal" and was making $1,750 a week when she left vaudeville. From 1910 to 1912 she had the lead with De Wolf Hopper on Broadway in *Matinee Idol* and later turned to the screen and appeared with Rudolph Valentino in *Lone Eagle* and Al Jolson in *Mammy.*

She also appeared in many other films including: *Air Circus; Lightnin'; State Fair; Dr. Bull; David*

Louise Dresser, right, with Will Rogers in *The County Chairman.*

Harum; The Scarlet Empress; The County Chairman; and *Maid of Salem.* She died April 24, 1965 at the Motion Picture Country House in Woodland Hills, California.

Ralph Dumke
1899-1964

Ralph Dumke was practically in every phase of the entertainment field, but probably gained his greatest popularity in the mid 1930s when he teamed with Ed East on radio in the comedy "Sisters of the Skillet."

He was born July 25, 1899 in Indiana. He left Notre Dame to become a song-and-dance man in vaudeville. Dumke was on the stage in the Los Angeles Civic Light Opera productions of *The Chocolate Soldier, Merry Widow* and *Rosalinda.* In 1946 he played the role of Cap'n Andy in the Broadway revival of *Show Boat.* He made his film

Ralph Dumke.

bow as "Tiny Duffy" in the award winning *All the King's Men* in 1949. He also appeared on many television shows. He died January 4, 1964.

A few of his other screen credits were: *Mystery Street; The Fireball; Carbine Williams; The Mississippi Gambler; Daddy Long Legs; Artists and Models; Invasion of the Body Snatchers; Solid Gold Cadillac; The Buster Keaton Story;* and *All in a Night's Work.*

Maude Eburne
1875-1960

Maude Eburne was a lovable, old character actress who added something to every film she was in. Her Canadian father was against her going on the stage even though that was her fondest desire. After his death, she became a newspaperwoman, but eventually got into stock in New York.

She appeared on Broadway with such stars as Will Rogers and Fred Stone. In 1918 she made her first film, *A Pair of Sixes* and she remained in Hollywood. One of her best known roles was in *Ruggles of Red Gap* in 1935 with Charles Laughton. She also played a running role as the housekeeper, Mrs. Hastings, in all of the Dr. Christian films.

Among her many other films were: *Poppy; Hollywood Cowboy; Sabotage; Meet Dr. Christian; You Belong to Me; Henry Aldrich; Editor; Rosie, The Riveter; I'm from Arkansas; The Suspect; Mother Wore Tights; Slippy McGee;* and *Arson, Inc.* She died October 8, 1960.

James Edwards
1912-1970

James Edwards began his acting career on Broadway in the controversial *Deep Are the Roots,* in which he played a romantic role opposite Barbara Bel Geddes. He was also in *Almost Faithful* and *Lady Passing Fair.*

During World War II, he was a lieutenant in the

Maude Eburne, center, with El Brendel and Carolina Cotton in *I'm from Arkansas*.

James Edwards, left, in *The Manchurian Candidate*.

United States Army. He had received a Bachelor's degree in psychology from Indiana University in 1938 and had participated in college dramatics. He made his motion picture debut in *Set-Up* in 1949. At one time he ran a dramatic school in Los Angeles and also wrote documentaries for David Wolper Productions.

His films included: *Bright Victory; Member of the Wedding; Caine Mutiny; Seven Angry Men; Manhandled; The Joe Louis Story; Phoenix City Story; Pork Chop Hill; Manchurian Candidate; Sandpiper;* and most notably, *Home of the Brave.* His last films included *Patton* and *Questions.* On January 4, 1970, he died of a heart attack in San Diego.

Jack Elam
1916-

Jack Elam started his career by agreeing to finance two low-budget films if he could play the heavy in each. This led to a long career of playing the wild-eyed, sneaky terrorist with a touch of cowardice that has kept him in demand for many years. Typical of his films were the ones made with James Stewart. In these, he was shot by Stewart, stabbed to death, trampled to death by a horse, and impaled by a pitchfork. As Elam explained, "The only question was how and where I'd be done in."

Jack Elam, right, with Dick Van Dyke in *Never a Dull Moment*.

He was born November 13, 1916 in Phoenix, Arizona. After college he became an accountant, auditor and manager of a hotel. He became one of the highest salaried auditors until afflicted by the acting bug. Elam took time out from his continuing screen villainy to play heroic roles in two television shows in which he starred for Warner Bros. In "Dakotas" he was a gunslinger turned deputy and in "Temple Huston" he was again on the side of the law. In the last few years he changed his image.

The rugged six-foot-two-inch Elam began sporting a beard and actually started having the audience on his side as his roles began to have a comic touch. He states "I enjoy the comic roles and the old-man roles very much, but I like to stock in one of my old-time heavies every once in a while just to sustain the image that got me where I am today....wherever that is."

His films include: *The Sundowners; Rawhide; Rancho Notorious; Never a Dull Moment; Ride Vaquero; Night Passage; The Comancheros; The Rare Breed; The Way West; Support Your Local Sheriff; Rio Lobo; The Wild Country;* and *Hannie Caulder.*

Robert Emhardt
1901-

Robert Emhardt was born in Indianapolis, Indiana, the son of C.J. Emhardt, lawyer, judge and onetime mayor of that city.

His early acting experience included Butler University Theatre, the London Academy of Dramatic Art (1937-1938) and repertoire on London's British Broadcasting Company. He came to Broadway in 1940 in *Battle of Angels* and appeared there in some twelve other plays until 1959. Emhardt has also appeared in some 125 productions in summer stock and over 250 television shows. He has no favorite medium when it comes to acting, but his favorite film role was that of the offbeat father in *The Group.*

Emhardt is married to the well-known English actress, Silvia Sideli. They have four children, two graduated from University of California at Los Angeles. He is actively engaged in St. Augustine's Episcopal Church of Santa Monica and the Boy Scouts of America. Hobbies include sports and the

Robert Emhardt.

ballet. Film credits in addition to *The Group* include: *I Hate Your Guts; Kid Galahad; The Iron Mistress; The Stranger; Where Were You When the Lights Went Out?; Underworld USA;* and *Three-Ten to Yuma.*

Julia Faye
1896-1966

Julia Faye was born in Richmond, Virginia, on September 24, 1896. She entered films in 1916 with D.W. Griffith and later moved to Famous Players—Lasky, where she became associated with Cecil B. DeMille and was for years a leading lady in his pictures, both silent and talking. Her credits included: *Male and Female; The Ten Com-*

mandments; King of Kings; Union Pacific; Northwest Mounted Police; Only Yesterday; Till We Meet Again; and *Samson and Delilah.* Her last appearance was in *The Last Buccaneer,* produced by Henry Wilcoxon for the DeMille Company in 1958. She died of cancer on April 6, 1966, in Hollywood.

Louise Fazenda
1895-1962

Louise Fazenda was in her heyday in Mack Sennett's Keystone comedies in 1917 with veterans Charlie Murray, Ben Turpin, Al St. John, Slim Summerville, and Sydney Chaplin. She began her career with Sennett in 1915 and became an accomplished comedienne. She engaged in daring stunts that no other female comic would try. In many films she was dragged by horses, tossed from dizzy

Louise Fazenda.

Julia Faye.

heights, and roughoused with man and beast in her descending bloomers which of course delighted her boss, Mr. Sennett. She remained with him until the early twenties when she shifted to features and continued to make a name for herself as an eccentric comedienne. When talkies arrived she continued in films to play character parts for most of the major studios. She died April 17, 1962 of a cerebral hemorrhage leaving her husband, producer Hal Wallis.

Her films included: *No, No Nanette; Gold Diggers of Broadway; Wonder Bar; Mountain Music; Colleen; First Lady; Swing Your Lady;* and *The Old Maid.*

Norman Fell.

Norman Fell
1924-

Norman Fell was born in Philadelphia, Pennsylvania. He didn't know what he wanted to do so, after finishing high school, he joined the United States Air Force, where he became an aerial gunner during World War II.

After his discharge he enrolled at Temple University graduating in 1950 with a BA degree in drama. Unable to find work in New York, he accepted the advice of Marlon Brando to study drama with the famed coach, Stella Adler. He also began working with Lee Strasberg in the Actors Studio.

Gradually, after a couple of years in various summer stock productions, he found his way into television. His guest television appearances have topped the four hundred mark. He has also co-starred in two series, "87th Precinct" and "Dan August."

Film roles came his way starting with his first motion picture *Pork Chop Hill.* Two of his favorite roles were in *The Graduate* and *If It's Tuesday, This Must Be Belgium.* Among his other films are: *Inherit the Wind; Catch 22; Oceans 11; Rat Race;* and *Bullitt.*

When not acting, Fell likes reading (biographies) and traveling.

Parker Fennelly (82)

Parker Fennelly was born of parents who were nonprofessionals in Northeast Harbor, Maine. Always stage struck, Fennelly participated in amateur theatricals in his hometown. After high school, he attended Island Powers School, Boston. From there he went out for two seasons on Chautauqua doing Shakespeare. This was followed by one season as a play reader on Lyceum. For a while he played stock in the middle west and then went into the army. Upon return to civilian life, Fennelly appeared on Broadway with such stars as Walter Huston in *Mister Pitt*; Frank Keenan in *Black Velvet*; and Roland Young in *The Queen's Husband.* Stock work in Washington, D.C. followed and then in 1929 he went into radio, playwriting, and finally films.

Radio and television have outnumbered Fennelly's film appearances, but he has to his film

Parker Fennelly.

credits: *Lost Boundaries; The Whistle at Eaton Falls; It Happened to Jane; Ma and Pa Kettle; Angel in My Pocket; How to Frame a Figg;* and *Pretty Poison.*

Fennelly married a former actress and they have twin daughters. He enjoys gardening and occasionally goes into New York to do Pepperidge Farm commercials. His favorite role was "Mr. Purdy," on Andy Griffith's television series, "Headmaster."

John Fiedler
1925-

Born in Plateville, Wisconsin, John Fiedler spent the first seven years of his life there and then moved to Milwaukee. After a turn in the navy he spent two years at the Neighborhood Playhouse in New York, graduating in 1947.

John Fiedler, center, with Richard Erdman and Henry Jones in *Rascal.*

For the next ten years, Fiedler appeared in many television shows and summer stocks. His first television performance was in "The Aldrich Family" in 1950. During this same time period he played in many off-Broadway and Broadway shows. Two of these were the hits, *A Raisin in the Sun* and *The Odd Couple*, both of which he did as films.

Mr. Fiedler's first film was *Twelve Angry Men* and among his other film credits are: *A Fine Madness* and *Girl Happy*. His hobby is bridge.

Edward Fielding
1879-1945

Edward Fielding was a native New Yorker and had a long career on Broadway after making his stage debut in London. When he returned to the United States he was seen in such plays as *Ghosts*; *Merchants of Glory*; *The Amazing Dr. Clitterhouse*; and many others. In 1939 he left the cast of *The Brown Danube* to appear with Leslie Howard in *Intermezzo* and he remained in Hollywood to appear in such films as *Rebecca*; *All This and Heaven Too*; *Kitty Foyle*; *Hold Back the Dawn*; *Beyond the Blue Horizon*; *Ten Gentlemen from West Point*; *The Major and the Minor*; *Mr. Lucky*; *Dead Man's Eyes*; *Belle of the Yukon*; and *The Beautiful Cheat*. He died at his home in Hollywood of a heart attack while mowing his lawn January 10, 1945.

Edward Fielding, right, with Acquanetta and Paul Kelly in *Dead Man's Eyes.*

Stanley Fields, center, with Gladys George and Loretta Young in *The Lady from Cheyenne*.

Stanley Fields
1883-1941

Stanley Fields was born Walter Agnew in Allegheny, Pennsylvania, May 20, 1883. He began his career as a singer in a George M. Cohan musical on Broadway. He played in vaudeville as a blackface comedian and on the stage he was a partner of Frank Fay. He was a rugged-looking individual who could be as sinister as the role required, but he was also adept at comedy. He was preparing to report to RKO for his role in *Lady Scarface* when he died of a heart attack on April 23, 1941.

His busy film career led to roles in: *Little Caesar*; *Girl Crazy*; *Island of Lost Souls*; *Strictly Dynamite*; *Baby Face Harrington*; *Mutiny on the Bounty*; *O'Malley of the Mounted*; *Maid of Salem*; *Wells Fargo*; *Hell's Kitchen*; and *The Lady from Cheyenne*.

James Finlayson
1887-1953

James Finlayson was the moustached menace to Laurel and Hardy in many of their films. He was born in Falkirk, Scotland on August 27, 1887. His father wanted him to join him in his iron foundry business but he rebelled and became an actor.

After some success on the English stage he came to America in 1912 in a Scottish comedy, *Bunty Pulls the Strings* and the show played Broadway for eighteen months. While on tour he stopped in Hollywood in 1916 and decided to stay.

Finlayson signed a contract with Mack Sennett and for three years played with the zany Keystone Kops. He then signed a four year contract with Hal Roach, followed by free lancing. He died at his Hollywood home October 9, 1953.

His films included: *Pack Up Your Troubles; Bonnie Scotland; The Bohemian Girl; Our Relations; Way Out West; Pick A Star; Blockheads; Hollywood Cavalcade; The Flying Deuces; Saps at Sea; To Be Or Not To Be; Yanks Ahoy;* and *When Comedy Was King.*

James Finlayson, right, with Oliver Hardy and Stan Laurel in *Big Business*.

Pat Flaherty
1903-1970

Pat Flaherty had the distinction of trying to teach two nonbaseball playing men to play baseball for their film roles. They were Gary Cooper who portrayed Lou Gehrig in *Pride of the Yankees* in 1942 and William Bendix who played Babe Ruth in *The Babe Ruth Story* in 1948. In addition to being a technical advisor on these two films as well as others he also appeared in over one hundred films as an actor.

He was born March 8, 1903 in Washington, D.C. and became a professional minor-league baseball player and a punter for the Chicago Bears in 1923.

When he retired from sports he became the vice-president of the legendary DeSylva, Brown, and Henderson music publishing firm and later heading his own music company. He went to Hollywood to open a music subsidiary for 20th Century-Fox, but this opportunity did not materialize. He turned to acting instead making his film debut in *Come on Marines* in 1934. He served in four wars, The Mexican Border Campaign in 1916, World War I and II, and was a Marine Corps Major in the Korean conflict. He died December 2, 1970 in New York of a heart attack.

Among his films were: *Chinatown Squad; Mutiny on the Bounty; My Man Godfrey; Legion of Lost Flyers; My Son, My Son; Sergeant York; Gentleman Jim; Best Years of Our Lives; Give My Regards to Broadway;* and *The Jackie Robinson Story.*

Pat Flaherty, right, with Minor Watson in *The Jackie Robinson Story*.

Joe Flynn.

Joe Flynn
1924-1974

Joe Flynn, well known for his portrayal of the gruff PT commander on television's "McHale's Navy," was born in Youngstown, Ohio.

Flynn began acting professionally at the age of six with Olsen and Johnson. During World War II he served as an entertainment specialist. In films since 1953, his first was *Rear Window* from which all his footage was cut when it was released.

His favorite role was "always his next" and the character he played "was always myself." Educated at the University of Notre Dame and the University of Southern California, Flynn, in addition to his acting, served as the Commissioner of Municipal Arts of the City of Los Angeles and a vice president of the Screen Actors Guild.

Well known in television and films, his many film credits included: *The Eddie Foy Story; Lover Come Back; Cry for Happy; The Last Time I Saw Archie; The Barefoot Executive; McHale's Navy; McHale's Navy Joins the Air Force; Son of Flubber; Super-Dad;* and *Now You See Him, Now You Don't.*

Wallace Ford in *Harvey*.

Wallace Ford
1898-1966

Wallace Ford, craggy-faced actor, was born Samuel Jones in London, England, and lived for a time in an orphanage after being separated from his parents. At an early age he was sent to a Toronto branch of the orphanage.

At eleven, after living in seventeen foster homes he ran away and joined a vaudeville troupe called the Winnipeg Kiddies, with whom he remained from 1911 to 1914. He then joined a friend named Wallace Ford and hoboed into the United States. A railroad car crushed that Ford to death and the actor-to-be took his friend's name, and found work in shoestring theatrical troupes and repertory companies.

Ford's career led him to Broadway and a number of plays including: *Abraham Lincoln; Abie's Irish Rose; Bad Girl;* and *Gypsy.* In 1932, he signed a movie contract with M-G-M, and his first film was with Joan Crawford in *Possessed.* Among his later movies were: *Breaking Point; Harvey;* and *Painting the Clouds with Sunshine.* The actor appeared in thirteen films directed by John Ford including *The Last Hurrah* and *The Informer.* His last picture was *A Patch of Blue.* He appeared in more than two hundred movies.

William Frawley
1893-1966

William Frawley had a most successful theatrical career that spanned vaudeville, Broadway musicals, films, and television.

Born in Burlington, Iowa, he toured in vaudeville and then appeared in a number of Broadway musicals. He then went to Hollywood, where for years he appeared as a character leading man under

William Frawley.

ents came from Russia at the turn of the century and none of the family was remotely involved with show business.

Attending the public schools in New York, Freed was graduated from Pennsylvania State University in 1940 with a B.S. degree in education. His early acting experience was gained in school productions and the Penn State Players.

Shortly after graduation he was admitted to the NYA Radio Workshop along with Carl Reiner, John Berry, and Mimi Benzell. He first appeared on Broadway in *Johnny 2X4* in 1942. This was followed by such Broadway shows as: *Strip for Action; One Touch of Venus; Kiss Them for Me;* and *Annie Get Your Gun.*

Freed's film career began in New York in the film *Carnegie Hall*. He moved to Hollywood in 1949 where he immediately became a character actor in great demand for movies and television.

His many movie roles include: *Keys to the City; No Way Out; Halls of Montezuma; Detective Story; Where the Sidewalk Ends; Red Mountain; Snows of*

contract to Paramount. He appeared in more than one hundred films. His screen debut came in 1933 in *Moonlight and Pretzels*. Other later pictures included: *Mother Wore Tights; Miracle on 34th Street; My Wild Irish Rose; Pretty Baby; Rhubarb; The Lemon Drop Kid; St. Louis Blues;* and *Kiss Tomorrow Goodbye.*

Very Irish in his ways, he was a great teller of tales, enjoyed cheerful company and a nip now and then. He was bluff and blustery, always with a twinkle in his eye and a jut to his jaw that characterized him as a tough cookie.

In later life, Frawley gained television fame through roles (Fred Mertz) on Lucille Ball's series and the "My Three Sons" show.

Bert Freed
1919-

Bert Freed was born in New York City. His par-

Bert Freed.

Kilimanjaro; Cobwebb; Desperate Hours; and *Billy Jack.*

In retrospect Freed says, "an evening spent with Chaplin and a lunch with Gable are among my most treasured memories." His hobby is contract bridge.

Dwight Frye
1899-1943

Dwight Frye had the distinction of playing prominent roles in two of the screen's greatest horror classics, both in the same year, 1931. In *Dracula* he portrayed the insect devouring "Renfield" and in *Frankenstein* he played "Fritz," the mad dwarf, responsible for substituting a criminal brain for the Frankenstein monster. He was born in Denver, Colorado and decided to become an actor after attending a touring stock company performance.

He left for New York and after catching on with road companies he landed on Broadway. Frye became a renowned Broadway actor and was a favorite with the critics. In 1930 he left for Hollywood and made his first film. He continued to appear in horror films throughout his career with only an occasional change of pace.

His pictures included: *Man to Man; The Vampire Bat; The Bride of Frankenstein; Alibi for Murder; The Man Who Found Himself; The Invisible Enemy; Gangs of Chicago; Frankenstein Meets the Wolf Man;* and *Dead Men Walk.*

Dwight Frye in *Dracula.*

Richard (Skeets) Gallagher
1890-1955

Skeets Gallagher was a song and dance man who ended up in Hollywood. He was born July 28, 1890 in Terre Haute, Indiana. He studied for two years at Rose Polytechnic Institute and then tried his hand at law at the University of Indiana.

He tired of this and played vaudeville in Chicago and then became a headliner on the Keith and Orpheum circuit. Gallagher made his New York debut on the legitimate stage in 1921 in *Up in the Clouds* and the next year reached Broadway in *Up She Goes*. He appeared in a number of musical comedies including *No, No Nanette* before going to Hollywood. His first film role was opposite W.C. Fields in *The Potters* in 1927. He appeared in many films the next few years and often was portrayed as a song and dance man.

Other films were: *Dance of Life; Let's Go Native; Social Lion; Bird of Paradise; Night Club Lady;*

Alice in Wonderland; In the Money; The Man I Marry; Espionage; Idiot's Delight; Brother Orchid; and *Duke of Chicago*. His last appearance was on the stage with Gloria Swanson in 1951 in *Three for Bedroom C*. He died May 22, 1955.

Claude Gillingwater
1870-1939

Claude Gillingwater was born on August 2, 1870 in Louisiana, Missouri. He had an extensive stage career starting with David Belasco; Gillingwater appeared on the New York stage for eight years. He made his film debut in 1921 appearing opposite Mary Pickford in *Little Lord Fauntleroy*. He was a very tall, thin actor with a perpetual frown and very much in demand. His last few years were marred by an injury, the death of his wife, and failing health. On November 1, 1939 he died of a self-inflicted bullet wound. His films included: *Daddy Long Legs; Ace of Aces; City Limits; Mississippi; A Tale of Two Cities; The Prisoner of Shark Island; Little Miss Broadway;* and *Cafe Society*.

Lucile Gleason
1888-1947

Lucile Gleason was born in Pasadena, California on February 6, 1888 and made her stage debut in 1904 in the *Merchant of Venice* and her New York debut in 1919. There weren't too many mother, father, and son combinations in films, but Lucile Gleason was an integral part of one of them. She married the famous comedian, James Gleason in 1906 while they were both appearing in a stock company run by her father. Two years later their son, Russell, was born and they eventually appeared together in the legitimate theater and they later switched to films. The Gleasons toured the country and appeared in three plays written and directed by her husband, *Is Zat So?; The Fall Guy;* and *The Shannons of Broadway*. James Gleason

Skeets Gallagher.

Claude Gillingwater, right, with Michael Whalen and Shirley Temple in *Poor Little Rich Girl*.

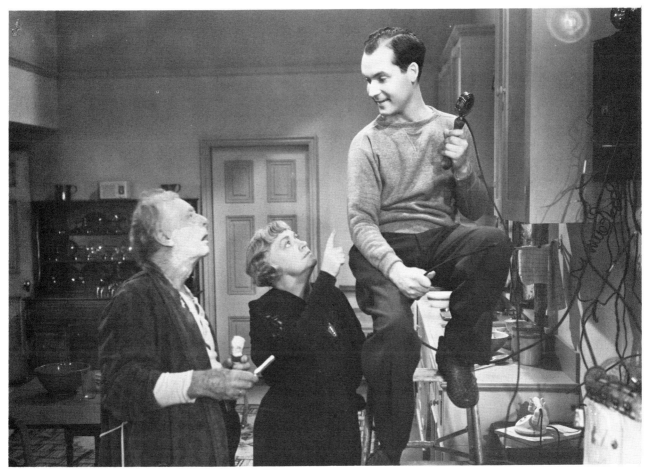

Lucile Gleason, center, with Harry Davenport and Russell Gleason in *The Higgins Family*.

went to Hollywood in 1929 as a film writer and soon they were acting together in films.

In addition to acting she was active in politics; in 1944 she was defeated as a candidate for the California Assembly. She was also a vice-president of Screen Actors Guild. She died in her sleep at her home in Brentwood May 17, 1947.

Among her films were: *Beloved; Klondike Annie; Rhythm on the Range; Red Light Ahead; First Lady; Nurse from Brooklyn; The Higgins Family; Covered Trailer; Grandpa Goes to Town; Lucky Partners;* and *She's in the Army.*

Bill Goodwin
1910-1958

Bill Goodwin was probably best known as a radio announcer. His good humored delivery, pleasant voice, and pleasing personality made him an integral part of the shows he announced. He was an announcer for "Blondie;" "Bob Hope;" "Eddie Cantor;" "Edgar Bergen;" and "Burns and Allen." His association with the latter lasted for twenty years.

He was born in San Francisco, July 28, 1910. He attended the Glen Taylor Military Academy in Alameda and the Santa Clara prep school. In 1930, after being in several school plays, he quit the University of California to become an actor in stock companies.

Goodwin found it tough to make a living as an actor during the depression so he joined a radio station in Sacramento where he became a twelve hour a day jack-of-all-trades. At the time he was in charge of production at a Hollywood station, then he moved to New York in 1934 and began his long association with George Burns and Gracie Allen.

His first film role was in *Let's Make Music* at RKO in 1940; this began an eighteen year career in films. His other films included: *Wake Island; So Proudly We Hail; Spellbound; The Jolson Story; Heaven Only Knows; Jolson Sings Again; The Life of Riley; Tea for Two; The First Time; Lucky Me;* and *Going Steady.* He was found dead in his automobile of an apparent heart attack May 9, 1958.

Bill Goodwin.

Leo Gorcey
1917-1969

Leo Gorcey was the son of Bernard Gorcey, the original Isaac Cohen in *Abie's Irish Rose.* Gorcey skyrocketed to attention in 1935 for his portrayal of "Spit" in the Broadway hit, *Dead End.* Two years later he was cast as the slum youngster in Samuel Goldwyn's movie version of the hit play.

Later, he and the other original "Deadenders," Billy Halop, Huntz Hall, Gabe Dell, Bobby Jordan, and Bernard Pumsley, were starred in *East Side Kids*, turned out by the old Monogram Studios. Playing the tough leader addicted to malapropisms, he headed the Bowery Boys and made many comedy features in the 1940s and 1950s. He appeared in such features as: *Crime School; Hell's Kitchen; Angels with Dirty Faces; Battle of City Hall;* and *Destroyer.*

Leo Gorcey in *Crime School*.

Gorcey, survived by his wife Mary, a son, and two daughters, had retired in 1956 to his ranch outside Los Molinos, California, one hundred miles above Sacramento. His death was preceeded by a long period of ill health.

William Gould
?-1960

William Gould started his film career in the Ken Maynard Western films for Universal in the early thirties. He could usually be found as the big boss or crooked cattleman. He continued his career in western films starring Tom Tyler, George O'Brien, or Jack Perrin. He later made the transition easily to other types of films and would portray a businessman, politician, warden, or an army officer. He studied engineering in college but decided to become an actor. Gould spent twenty years in stock and sometime on the radio before his breakthrough to films. During World War II he produced army camp shows. He died March 29, 1960.

His films included: *Gun Justice*; *Wheels of Destiny*; *Hard Rock Harrigan*; *Mr. Wong*; *Detective*; *Women in the Wind*; *Dr. Christian Meets the Women*; *The Strange Case of Dr. Rx*; *Murder in the Big House*; *The Adventures of Mark Twain*; *Texas Panhandle*; *The Devil Thumbs a Ride*; and *The Winner's Circle*.

William Gould, right, with Jean Willes in *The Winner's Circle*.

Alexander Granach
1890-1945

Alexander Granach came to the United States in 1938 from Europe. He translated the pioneer anti-Nazi play, *Professor Matlock* into Yiddish, produced it and played the lead three hundred times in Poland early in the Hitler regime. He then decided it would be best to leave Europe.

He was born April 18, 1890 in Poland and studied for the stage at Max Reinhardt's school in Berlin. Granach was on the dramatic stage in Shakespearean roles in many European countries and appeared in German and Russian films. His first film role in the United States was as one of Greta Garbo's comrades in *Ninotchka* in 1939.

Other films in which he appeared were: *A Man Betrayed; So End Our Night; Joan of Paris; Wrecking Crew; Hangmen also Died; Mission to Moscow; For Whom the Bells Toll; Three Russian Girls; Voice in the Wind; The Hitler Gang;* and *The Seventh Cross.* His last role was on the New York stage as "Tomasino" in *A Bell for Adano.* He died March 14, 1945.

Harrison Greene
1884-1945

Harrison Greene was born January 18, 1884 in Portland, Oregon. He was very active in vaudeville touring the circuits with his wife in an act known as Greene and Parker. He also performed with Weber and Fields and Kolb and Dill in various musical shows. When he came to Hollywood in 1929 he became not only an actor but also a talent scout. He died September 28, 1945.

A few of his film credits were: *International House; Riot Squad; The Singing Cowboy; The Sea Spoilers; A Bride for Henry; Mr. Boggs Steps Out; Born To Be Wild; Career; The Honeymoon's Over; You Can't Fool Your Wife;* and *Between Two Women.*

Dabs Greer
1917-

Though born in Fairview, Missouri, Dabs Greer considers Anderson, Missouri, his "home." An only child, his father was a pharmacist, his mother a speech teacher.

Greer's first stage experience was in a Children's Theatre production of *Cinderella* in 1925. It continued periodically throughout his school years and college. A graduate of Drury College, Springfield, Missouri, in 1939, he became head of the drama department and Little Theatre in Mountain Grove, Missouri, from 1940 to 1943. He then went to the staff of the Pasadena Playhouse as actor, instructor and administrator from 1943 to 1950.

His first film experience came in 1948 in *The Black Book (Reign of Terror).* To date he has appeared in eighty-nine theatrical features and 433 television shows. His film credits include: *House of Wax; Trouble along the Way; Bitter Creek; Seven Angry Men; Pawnee; The Lone Texan; Showdown; Shenandoah;* and *Affair with a Stranger.*

Alexander Granach, right, with John Wayne in *A Man Betrayed*.

Huntz Hall
1920-

Huntz Hall was the dumb-witted member of a gang of good-natured hoodlums who captivated

Harrison Greene, left, with Edward Ellis and John Archer in *Career*.

Dabbs Greer, second from left, with Mary Jo Tarola, Jane Darwell, and Jean Simmons in *Affair with a Stranger*.

audiences from 1937 through 1957. Usually known as "Sach" he murdered the English language, was kicked around a lot, and wore a silly baseball cap with the brim turned upward. Through the years the gang was known as "The Dead End Kids," "The Little Tough Guys," "The East Side Kids" or "The Bowery Boys," and can still be seen on television.

He was born in New York City, attended St. Stephen's Grammar school, and went to the famed Professional Children's school. He was on the old Bobby Benson's "Adventures" on radio; in 1935 Martin Gabel got him a job in *Dead End* on Broadway, he spent eighteen months there. In 1937 he went to Hollywood and appeared in the film version of *Dead End* with Leo Gorcey, Billy Halop, Bobby Jordan, Gabe Dell, and Bernard Pumsley.

In addition to film roles he also played in three serials at Universal, *Junior G-Men*, 1940; *Sea Raiders*, 1941; and *Junior G-Men of the Air*, 1948. In 1971 he was in the short-lived television series "The Chicago Teddy Bears."

John Halliday in *The Mystery Woman*.

Huntz Hall.

His film work includes: *Crime School; Angels with Dirty Faces; Hell's Kitchen; Bowery Blitzkrieg; A Walk in the Sun; Spook Busters; Blonde Dynamite; Tell It to the Marines; High Society; In the Money;* and *Gentle Ben.*

John Halliday
1880-1947

John Halliday was one of the most distinguished-looking actors on the screen. He was born in Brooklyn on September 14, 1880 and spent his childhood in England where he studied mining engineering.

He served with the British Army in the Boer War, then came back to America and made a fortune as boss of the Jumbo Mine in Goldfield,

Kenneth Harlan, right, with **Mary Ainsley** in *Pride of the Bowery*.

Nevada only to lose it later on with bad investments. While at the mining camp he had his first taste of show business presenting Gilbert and Sullivan's Operetta *Pinafore* to the miners. He later performed at the Opera House in Sacramento and toured the Far East and Australia.

In 1912 showman William A. Brady offered him a part in the smash hit *The Whip;* in 1915 he began his Broadway career.

He entered films in 1930 and appeared in: *Captain Applejack; Finishing School; The Witching Hour; Mystery Woman; The Melody Lingers On; Peter Ibbetson; Desire; Hollywood Boulevard; Intermezzo;* and *The Philadelphia Story.* Halliday died in Honolulu (where he had made his home since 1939) on October 17, 1947.

Kenneth Harlan
1895-1967

Kenneth Harlan was a dashing leading man who played with the top players in silent films. He was born July 26, 1895 in Boston, Massachusetts. He made his stage debut at the age of seven and was a dancer in vaudeville. He entered films in 1917 in D.W. Griffith's *Betsy's Burglar.* He went on to a long career as a popular matinee idol opposite such ladies of the screen as: Mary Pickford, Constance Talmadge, and Dorothy Dalton. He remained active in films in the sound era in supporting roles retiring in 1944. He then turned to the restaurant business and later became a Hollywood agent who booked stripteasers. He was married and divorced six times, one of his wives was actress Marie Prevost. He died in Sacramento, California March 6, 1967.

His motion picture credits included: *Air Police*; *Cappy Ricks Returns*; *China Clipper*; *San Francisco*; *Marked Woman*; *Law of the Texan*; *Slightly Honorable*; *A Little Bit of Heaven*; *Pride of the Bowery*; *Foreign Agent*; and *The Underdog*.

Otis Harlan
1864-1940

In the 1930s if a director was looking for an elderly gentleman to play a kindhearted role chances are he would choose Otis Harlan.

He was born December 29, 1864 in Zanesville, Ohio. He made his stage debut as a romantic young man in *The Hole in the Ground*, in New York. He later appeared with Weber and Fields, Elsie Janis, and Anna Held. Harlan reportedly was the first performer to sing Irving Berlin's "Alexander's Ragtime Band" to an audience on the New York Stage. His last stage role was as Judge Splint in *Ninety in the Shade* in 1914. He then entered films. Harlan suffered a stroke in 1938, and retired from films the following year. He died January 20, 1940 in Martinsville, Indiana.

Otis Harlan, left, with Lyle Talbot in *Chinatown Squad*.

His films included: *King of Jazz*; *Air Eagles*; *Partners*; *The Big Shot*; *Telegraph Trail*; *The Old-Fashioned Way*; *Chinatown Squad*; *A Midsummer Night's Dream*; *Can This Be Dixie?*; *Western Gold*; and *Mr. Boggs Steps Out*.

Paul Hartman
1904-1973

Paul Hartman, a rubber-faced, rubber-legged comedian, formed with his wife, Grace, one of the most delightful comic ballroom-dancing acts in show business.

Hartman's birth and stage premiere were practically one and the same, since he made his first appearance when only six weeks old at the Tivoli Opera House in San Francisco. His father, Ferris Hartman, was known as the "Ziegfeld of the Pacific Coast."

Though he entered the University of California at the age of eighteen, he quickly returned to show business starting out as a dance partner with Edna Malone, then amusing night club audiences with such partners as: Ginger Rogers; Fay Emerson; Nancy Walker; and his wife, Grace. They played vaudeville theatres throughout the country and were headlined in *Red, Hot and Blue* (their Broadway stage debut). In 1948, the Hartman's performance in *Angel in the Wings* won them the Antoinette Perry and Donaldson awards.

Hollywood beckoned Hartman in 1952; subsequently he appeared in such films as: *Forty-Five Fathers*; *Inherit the Wind*; *Soldier in the Rain*; *Those Calloways*; *How to Succeed in Business without Really Trying*; and *Luv*. He also established a reputation for his varied appearances on television. He was a favorite on "Mayberry RFD."

Rondo Hatton
1894-1946

Karloff, Lugosi, and the Chaneys were the most

Paul Hartman, left, with Ed Wynn in *Those Calloways*.

famous of those who plied their trade in horror films. As great as they were they did need makeup for their roles. Rondo Hatton wasn't much of an actor, but he was frightening without any help. He was born April 22, 1894 in Hagerstown, Maryland, and was a victim of acromegaly which gave him gruesome features. He played minor roles in several films, but received top billing in *The Brute Man*, his last film. He starred as the killer ("The Creeper") who was disfigured by acid while in college and sought vengeance on former school chums. He died February 2, 1946 of a heart attack, two months before the film was released.

Other features included: *The Ox Bow Incident*; *In Old Chicago*; *The Pearl of Death*; *Jungle Captive*; *The Spider Woman Strikes Back*; and *House of Horrors*.

Sessue Hayakawa
1890-1973

A leading figure of the silent screen, ordained Zen priest, painter, author, 1957 Oscar nominee, Sessue Hayakawa's career had many stages.

Named Kintaro Hayakawa at his birth (on the island of Honshu in Japan) he was descended from a long aristocratic line. His father was the governor of a Japanese prefecture. Hayakawa was brought up in the strict warrior code of Bushido with plans for a Navy career. A ruptured eardrum ended these hopes, so his family sent him to the University of Chicago in 1909 to learn banking. He was

Rondo Hatton.

Sessue Hayakawa.

graduated in 1913 with a degree in political science.

Hayakawa was to return to Japan, but stopped in Los Angeles and became involved in the Japanese Theatre. At this time he was signed for his first film *Typhoon*. DeMille's 1916 film, *The Cheat*, firmly established his career.

With good looks and expressive gestures, Mr. Hayakawa was perfectly suited to bringing silent optics to life. In 1919, he founded the Haworth Pictures Corp. By the early thirties, with the arrival of talking pictures, his career began to wane. The war trapped him in Europe where he managed to live on an income from painting.

In 1949, Hayakawa returned to the United States to appear with Humphry Bogart in *Tokyo Joe*. Subsequently, he had other roles in a variety of war movies. He regarded his role as Colonel Saito in *The Bridge on the River Kwai* (Academy nomination) as the high point of his career. Despite his reputation as a "heavy," he played a variety of roles. His talking picture credits included: *Yoshiwara; Macao; Green Mansions; The Big Wave; The Geisha Boy; Three Came Home;* and Disney's *Swiss Family Robinson*.

Vinton Hayworth
1906-1970

Vinton J. Hayworth began his acting career in Washington in 1925. He is best remembered as "Jack Arnold" in the "Myrt and Marge" radio series, which ran for six years.

He was a founder of AFRA (now AFTRA), when it was a radio union. In the late 1930s he appeared in many pictures at 20th Century-Fox and his only television credit in Hollywood was with *I Dream of Jeannie.*

His film credits include: *The Girl He Left Behind; The Great Man; Police Dog Story;* and *Chamber of Horrors.*

Myron Healey
1923-

During the peak of his career Myron Healey was at his best in the role of a hired killer who obviously enjoyed his work. Some of his more treacherous roles even suggested a slight mental disturbance.

He was born Myron Daniel Healey on June 8, 1923 in Petaluma, California. His father was Doctor Daniel Healey, a noted proctologist. In the mid-thirties he performed as a child singer on radio, gave violin, dance and piano concert recitals. He became interested in acting while in high school and participated in plays there and in junior college.

After studying under famed actress Maria Ouspenskaya in 1941 he appeared in several plays and also appeared in musicals for the Armed Forces Victory Committee. He signed an M-G-M contract in August of 1942 and appeared in their "Crime Does Not Pay" series. He served as a navigator in the Army Air Corps during World War II and twice was awarded the air medal.

Following the war he resumed his career both in the movies and on many television shows. In 1950 he authored the screenplay for *Outlaw Gold* and in 1951 *Colorado Ambush* for Monogram. Since 1943 he has appeared in over five hundred films for theatrical and television release. Among his favorite roles he numbers the "Sheriff" in *Son of Belle Starr* and "Rault" in *Monsoon.* His films include: *Laramie; I Killed Geronimo; The Longhorn; The Maverick; Silver Lode; Calling Homicide; The Unearthly; Quantrill's Raiders; Convicts 4; Journey to Shiloh;* and *True Grit.*

Vinton Hayworth in *Without Orders*.

Ted Healy
1896-1937

Ted Healy was the leader of a gang of ruffians known as the "racketeers." The act in vaudeville and musical comedies was an unbelievably violent affair. He would get his partners in an argument and while they battled it out he became an onlooker. The act was later called "Ted Healy and the Stooges" and later "The Three Stooges" went on to make many short subjects for Columbia.

He was born in Houston, Texas on October 1, 1896. He quit school and went on the stage, first burlesque, then vaudeville where he did blackface

Myron Healey, left, with Art Baker and James Lydon in *Hot Rod*.

Ted Healy, left, in *Variety Show*.

imitations. He appeared in the 1925 edition of Earl Carroll's vanities. His first appearance in films was *Soup to Nuts* with the Stooges in 1930. He made a few Hal Roach comedies and in 1933 he went to feature films completely.

On December 19, 1937 he was involved in a fight at the Trocadero Night Club in Hollywood and died the next day. An autopsy was ordered but it was determined that he died of a heart attack.

Some of his pictures were: *Dancing Lady; Lazy River; Death on the Diamond; Reckless; Murder in the Fleet; San Francisco; Speed; Sing, Baby Sing; Good Old Soak; Hollywood Hotel;* and *Varsity Show.*

Eileen Heckart
1919-

Eileen Heckart whom Kenneth Tynan once described as "the best actress alive," was born in Columbus, Ohio. Miss Heckart attended Ohio State University, where she was active in campus drama groups. After graduation in 1942 she went to New York where one year later she got her first break in a Blackfriars Guild production, *Tinker's Damn.*

She began in television when everyone else was beginning. Playing every type role, it proved to be great training. In films since 1956 her performances include: *Miracle in the Rain; The Bad Seed; Hot Spell; Heller in Pink Tights; Up the Down Staircase; No Way to Treat a Lady; Bus Stop;* and *My Six Loves.*

Specializing in playing lonely, alcoholic, kooky or wise-cracking women, Miss Heckart has been nominated for the Tony five times and the Oscar once before she won it for best supporting actress in *Butterflies Are Free.*

Mainly an actress on the stage—*The Bad Seed; Dark at the Top of the Stairs; I Can't Hear You When the Water's Running*—her career has wended its way through innumerable theatrical productions, television shows and films. Known as an "actor's actor," Eileen Heckart says she feels most comfortable working on the stage.

O.P. Heggie
1876-1936

O.P. Heggie was one of those players (such as Walter Brennan or Edgar Buchanan) who always were able to project an illusion of age. He was only forty-two years old when he played a ninety year old poet; he always seemed to be much older than he really was.

He was born September 17, 1876 in Angaston, South Australia and was brought up in the outposts of civilization. He was educated at Winham College in Adelaide and attended the Conservatory of Music with the idea of becoming a singer. O.P. Heggie tried his hand at law, but gave that up for the stage in 1899. He made his stage debut in London in 1906, and came to the United States in 1907. He entered films in 1927 and became one of the better character actors. After finishing a prominent role in *Prisoner of Shark Island* he died of pneumonia February 7, 1936.

His other films included: *The Mysterious Dr. Fu Manchu; The Vagabond King; Sunny; East Lynne; Devotion; Zoo in Budapest; Midnight; Count of Monte Cristo; Anne of Green Gables; Bride of Frankenstein; Ginger;* and *A Dog of Flanders.*

Howard Hickman
1880-1949

Howard C. Hickman was born February 9, 1880 in Columbia, Missouri. He made his stage debut with Robert Mantell in 1903 and in 1906 he married film actress Bessie Barriscale. They starred the following year on the stage in *Rose of the Rancho.* His first film role was as an extra in Cecil B. DeMille's *Rose of the Rancho* in 1914 in which his wife starred. He made many films thereafter well into the 1940s. Early in his career he turned to directing for Thomas Ince, but returned to acting. He died in Los Angeles on December 31, 1949.

A few of his screen credits were: *Mystery Liner; Jimmy the Gent; Fury; Western Gold; Start Cheering; Espionage Agent; Gone with the Wind; It All Came True; Cheers for Miss Bishop; Belle Starr; Watch on the Rhine;* and *Libeled Lady.*

Eileen Heckart in *Up the Down Staircase*.

O. P. Heggie in *Ginger*.

Howard Hickman, second from left, with Spencer Tracy
and Hal K. Dawson in *Libeled Lady*.

William Hopper
1915-1970

William Hopper, who played Perry Mason's friend and investigator, was the only child of the Hollywood columnist, Hedda Hopper, and DeWolf Hopper.

Hopper got his first film part in 1936 in *Sissy* with Grace Moore. He appeared in a number of films for Warner Brothers and 20th Century Fox. Besides roles in films, Mr. Hopper appeared in a number of television dramas. He is best known for his character of Paul Drake on the "Perry Mason" television series, in which he appeared for nine seasons, starting in 1957. *HEART ATTACK (heavy smoker)*

His film credits include: *Track of the Cat; Footloose Heiress; Over the Goal; Torchy Blane; 20 Million Miles to Earth;* and his last film assignment, *Myra Breckinridge.*

Arthur Housman
1889-1942

Arthur Housman was one of the two great screen "drunks." The other one was Jack Norton and like Norton he was a teetotaler in real life. Housman could be found staggering around in many films throughout the 1920s and 1930s. He was particularly prominent in the Laurel and Hardy films.

He was born in New York October 10, 1889. His first acting experience was on the stage; he switched to films in 1912 working for Edison, Essanay, and Selig Companies. Sound did not hamper his career as he was not only a visual drunk, but added slurred dialogue to his inebriated state. He died April 7, 1942 in Los Angeles of pneumonia.

His credits included: *Officer O'Brien; Girl of the Golden West; Night Life in Reno; Movie Crazy; She Done Him Wrong; Mrs. Wiggs of the Cabbage Patch; Paris in Spring; Diamond Jim; Riffraff;* and *Step Lively, Jeeves.*

William Hopper in *20 Million Miles to Earth*.

Shemp Howard
1895-1955

Shemp Howard will be remembered for his work with the zany "Three Stooges," but he appeared independently in many other films. He was born Sam Howard in Brooklyn on March 4, 1895.

In the early 1920s, Shemp and his brother Moe joined Ted Healy's vaudeville act. In 1925 they were joined by Larry Fine and went on tour with an act based on slapstick and violence and were known as "Ted Healy and his Stooges." They made their film debut in 1930 in *Soup to Nuts.* Healy left the act for better things. Columbia signed Shemp as a featured player; he was replaced by his brother "Curly" in "The Three Stooges." When Curly became very ill, Shemp replaced him. Shemp continued his work as one of the crazy trio who made 190 short subjects for Columbia from 1934 through 1958. Shemp Howard died of a heart attack in Hollywood (on the way home from an evening at the

Arthur Housman, center, with Oliver Hardy and Stan Laurel in *Our Relations*.

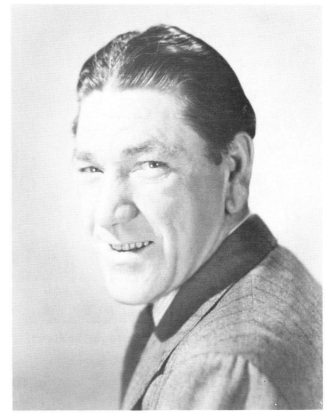

Shemp Howard.

prize fights in Hollywood Legion Stadium) on November 11, 1955.

His feature films included: *Hollywood Round Up; The Leather Pushers; Give Us Wings; The Bank Dick; Buck Privates; The Invisible Woman; In the Navy; Hold That Ghost; Hellzapoppin; Mississippi Gambler; Pittsburgh;* and *It Aint Hay.*

Walter Huston
1884-1950

Walter Huston was born Walter Houghston on April 6, 1884 in Toronto, Canada. Although he disliked school he did enjoy dramatics; in 1902, at the age of eighteen, he began acting on the New York stage. He left the stage, and from 1903 to 1908 he was engaged in engineering work. He returned to the stage in 1909 playing in his own vaudeville acts and occasionally writing songs and lyrics. He came to Broadway in 1924 for the title role of "Mr. Pitt." Huston had a long career on the stage; one of his greatest successes was the title role "Dodsworth."

He started his film career as a tall, rugged leading man and gradually became one of the best character actors on the screen. He was nominated for "Best Actor" in 1936 for his performance as "Sam Dodsworth" in *Dodsworth.* In 1942 he was nomimated for best supporting actor as "Jerry Cohan" in *Yankee Doodle Dandy.* He finally won an Oscar in 1948 as the hard-bitten prospector "Howard" in *The Treasure of Sierra Madre.* The film was written and directed by his son, John Huston.

Although his fame as an actor was well known, his rendition of "September Song" was never equaled by any recording artist. His last film was *The Furies* for Paramount; he was scheduled for the starring role in *Mr. 880,* the eccentric New York counterfeiter. The role went to Edmund Gwenn when Huston died of a heart attack April 7, 1950.

A few of his screen credits were; *Abraham Lincoln; Law and Order; The Prizefighter and the Lady; Of Human Hearts; All That Money Can Buy; Swamp Water; The Outlaw; Mission to Moscow; Dragon Seed;* and *Duel in the Sun.*

Walter Huston, right, with Judith Anderson in *The Furies*.

Jack Ingram
1902-1969

Jack Ingram specalized in being the villain in countless serials and westerns. He was born in Chicago, Illinois, and spent vacations on a farm in Wisconsin where he learned to ride. During World War I, he discovered while in training camps that he had the ability to entertain. After service he toured the country with the Mae West stage shows. In 1929 he was signed by Paramount; it was the beginning of a long career as a stuntman and villain.

In 1944 he married Eloise Fullerton, a writer; they purchased the Charlie Chaplin two hundred acre ranch in the Santa Monica mountains. They turned the ranch into a motion-picture location ranch with seventy-five buildings. It was used for

Jack Ingram in *Superman*.

a musician, playing her first piano recital in London when she was ten years old. She continued her musical career until her father died and then decided to become an actress.

She made her stage debut in the United States (1912) in *The Father*; George Bernard Shaw chose her to play in his *Candida*. On Broadway she played Queen Margaret in John Barrymore's *Richard III*. Although she appeared in many other stage plays, she also was a book reviewer for the *New York Times*. She brought her rich theatrical training to the screen in 1936, but didn't really make an impression until 1944 when she played the hateful badgering wife of Charles Laughton in *The Suspect*.

Other films that she scored heavily were: *The Corn is Green* and *Three Strangers*. She also appeared in *Pursuit to Algiers*; *Pillow of Death*; *Scarlett Street*; *The Verdict*; *That Brennan Girl*; *Johnny Belinda*; *The Robe*; and *Elephant Walk*. She died April 6, 1959.

the filming of Roy Rogers, Cisco Kid, and Lone Ranger television films. He later sold the ranch, bought a yacht and sailed up and down the coast in semiretirement. He rented the boat to the television producers of "Sea Hunt."

Jack Ingram died February 20, 1969; he will be long remembered by devotees of the serial.

His films included: *The Lonely Trail*; *Frontier Scout*; *Boom Town*; *Lone Star Trail*; *Range Law*; *The Jade Mask*; *The Strawberry Roan*; *Short Grass*; *Cave of Outlaws*; and *Utah Blaine*.

Rosalind Ivan in *The Suspect*.

Bud Jamison
1894-1944

William "Bud" Jamison was born in Vallejo, California on February 15, 1894. He spent four years in vaudeville and in stock companies; he entered films with Charlie Chaplin as a comedian,

Rosalind Ivan
1879-1959

Rosalind Ivan was born in London, England, the daughter of an accountant. She began her career as

Bud Jamison, left, with Curly Howard, Larry Fine, and Moe Howard.

in 1914. He also appeared in Harold Lloyd comedies. Jamison was usually found in a big top hat and wore a large, dark moustache. He played in many other short subjects and feature films; it was surprising how often he turned up as a cop, particularly in *The Three Stooges* short subjects for Columbia where he made at least fifty appearances as their foil. He finished his character part in *Nob Hill* on September 28, 1944, became ill and died two days later.

His motion picture credits included: *Hurry Call; Make Me A Star; Come and Get It; Ticket to Paradise; Melody of the Plains; See My Lawyer; Slightly Honorable; Captain Caution; True to Life;* and *L'il Abner*.

Soledad Jiminez
1874-1966

Soledad Jiminez was one of the real veterans of motion pictures. She appeared in the original version of *Carmen* in 1915 with Geraldine Farrar, and continued in many silents. She had a prominent role in one of the first talking westerns in 1929, *In Old Arizona*. John Ford consistently used her in many of his films. She was born February 28, 1874 in Santander, Spain; she died October 17, 1966 in the Motion Picture Country House where she had been a resident for six years.

Soledad Jiminez, left, with Henry Hull in *The Return of the Cisco Kid*.

Then, in 1950 he landed a role in *The Solid Gold Cadillac* which led to television from 1950 to 1953 and over two hundred shows. In 1952 he went to Hollywood to play in *The Lady Says No*. Other pictures include: *Taxi*; *This Is the Army*; *The Bad Seed*; *The Girl He Left Behind*; *Vertigo*; and *Cash McCall*.

His favorite stage portrayal was Elwood in *Harvey*. His favorite hobby is painting portraits and his favorite screen stars were Charles Coburn and Marilyn Monroe.

Some of her many films included: *Romance of the Rio Grande*; *The Arizona Kid*; *Broken Wing*; *Bordertown*; *Under the Pampas Moon*; *Robin Hood of El Dorado*; *Forbidden Valley*; *Return of the Cisco Kid*; *South of the Rio Grande*; and *Carnival in Costa Rica*.

Henry Jones
1912-

Henry Jones got started as an actor because he didn't have the money to follow his chosen profession, law. Born in Philadelphia, he attended the Academy of Notre Dame, St. Joseph's Prep, and St. Joseph's College.

Active in school productions, it was natural he should think of earning a living at acting after he met with little success as a salesman. He began his career with the Hedgerow Repertory Theatre outside Philadelphia in 1936. He went directly from there to Broadway, making his debut in 1938 in Maurice Evans *Hamlet*. There followed parts in *Henry IV*; *The Village Green*; and *My Sister Eileen*.

In 1942 Jones was inducted into the army appearing in their show, *This Is the Army*. Discharged in 1945, there then came the low spot in his career.

Henry Jones in *Angel Baby*.

Nicholas Joy
1884-1964

Nicholas Joy was a tall, debonair actor known for his comedy roles in both the theatre and on the screen. He was born in Paris, France, January 31,

Nicholas Joy, right, with Lou Costello in *Abbott and Costello Meet the Killer*.

1884 of British parents. He studied at London's Royal Academy of Dramatic Arts and appeared in his first stage play in 1910 called *A Butterfly on the Wheel* in London. He was first seen on Broadway in 1912 in *Henry V*. He was very versatile and was in many Broadway productions in a variety of roles in over one hundred plays. He also appeared in films and on television.

His screen roles included: *Daisy Kenyon; A Gentleman's Agreement; The Fuller Brush Man; Joan of Arc; Larceny; Bride of Vengeance; The Great Gatsby; Song of Surrender; Here Comes the Groom; Desk Set;* and *Abbott and Costello Meet the Killer*. He died March 16, 1964 in Philadelphia.

Charles Judels
1881-1969

Judels was born on August 17, 1881 in Amsterdam, Holland. He was a third generation in a family of actors, a tradition which has deep roots in the soil. His grandfather owned several theatres throughout Holland and starred in his own plays. Judels' father combined his love of the theatre with his love of music. He was stage manager for the Metropolitan Opera in New York for thirty-five years. He was also a stage director and produced

Charles Judels, right, with Ann Sothern in *Gold Rush Maisie*.

such hits as *Artists and Models*; *Gay Paree*; *A Night in Spain*; and eighty-seven farces, comedies, and dramas. In 1928 he was signed by Fox to direct Movietone.

In addition to being the model and voice of the cockney coachman in *Pinnochio*, some of his many films included: *The Florentine Dagger*; *The Plainsman*; *The Great Ziegfeld*; *San Francisco*; *Ebb Tide*; *Maytime*; *Marry the Girl*; *Love and Hisses*; *Bitter Sweet*; *It All Came True*; *Gold Rush Maisie*; *Career Girl*; and *A Bell For Adano*. He died on February 14, 1969.

Ian Keith
1899-1960

Ian Keith was born February 27, 1899 in Boston, Massachusetts. He attended the American Academy of Dramatic Arts in New York and he toured in stock and Shakespearean repertoire. He first appeared on Broadway in 1921 when William Faversham engaged him in *The Silver Fox*. His first leading role was as "Orlando" in *As You Like It* in

1923. In his thirty-nine years in the theatre he had appeared in more than 350 roles including Shakespearean parts in *Macbeth, Lear, Hamlet,* and *Othello.*

He began his film career in *Love's Wilderness* in 1924 and appeared in many silent films concurrent with his stage roles. He continued his film work in sound films and was active in a wide variety of roles. He also was prominent in television plays. He was married four times including marriages to actresses Blanche Yurka and Ethel Clayton. While appearing in "The Andersonville Trial" he died of a heart attack March 26, 1960.

Some of his many films included: *The Big Trail; Cleopatra; The Crusades; The Buccaneer; All This and Heaven Too; The Sea Hawk; Five Graves to Cairo; Valley of the Zombies; Nightmare Alley; Prince of Players; New York Confidential;* and *The Ten Commandments.*

DeForest Kelly

54(1979)

DeForest Kelley was born in Atlanta, Georgia, the son of a Baptist minister. At age seventeen, after graduation from high school he traveled to Long Beach, California, to visit relatives. Kelley decided to move there and enter show business.

In California, Kelley joined the Long Beach

Ian Keith, center, with **Lee Tracy** in *The Pay-Off*.

112

Lew Kelly
1879-1944

DeForest Kelley.

Lew Kelly was one of the finest burlesque comedians. He was a featured comedian for the "Behman Shows" and "Follies of the Day" in the era of refined burlesque. He created the role of the lovable hophead who was under the influence of a swig of the bamboo or sniffle of "nose candy." When burlesque got out of hand and became in his words "dirt shows" he left and turned his attention to musical comedies for the Shuberts.

Lew Kelly was born in St. Louis August 24, 1879 and began his career in stock and vaudeville before entering burlesque.

He entered films in 1929 and was active until his death June 10, 1944. Some of his films were: *Strange People; Six of a Kind; Diamond Jim; Death from a Distance; Forlorn River; Man from Music Mountain; Flirting with Fate; Lady of Burlesque; Taxi; Mister;* and *Gold Town.*

Theatre Group and formed a radio group with friends, while supplementing his income as an elevator operator. During the war a Paramount talent scout spotted him in a navy training film, and, after his discharge offered him a screen test which in turn led to a contract.

His first role was in *Fear in the Night*, a low budget film that turned out to be a box-office sleeper. In 1948, after two and one half years with the studio, he headed for New York to gain experience in stock, stage, and television.

Upon his return to California in 1953, he was quickly re-established in the film capital. Numerous television appearances followed in the major programs and series. Among Kelley's motion picture credits are: *Tension at Table Rock; Gunfight at the O.K. Corral; Raintree County; The Law and Jake Wade; Warlock;* and *Where Love Has Gone.*

Despite his appearances in such films and numerous television appearances, Kelley remains best remembered for his role as Dr. McCoy on the television series, "Star Trek."

Pert Kelton
1907-1968

Miss Kelton was born on a farm near Great Falls, Montana. Born of a vaudeville couple, Miss Kelton started in show business at the age of three, changing program cards and singing in her parents' act. She appeared in the act until she was 12. Miss Kelton made her legitimate bow in 1925 in *Sunny* and later *Five O'Clock Girl.* Her first appearance in films was in 1929 in *Sally.* Following her first film, she played various roles in other pictures.

Miss Kelton was the original stage wife of Jackie Gleason on his *Honeymooners* television sketches. She also did many roles in radio. In her work as an actress on Broadway, in films and on television, Miss Kelton was the complete professional. Her film credits include: *The Music Man* and *Billy Bright.*

Lew Kelly, right, with Doris Nolan in *The Man I Marry*.

Pert Kelton, center, with George Givot, Max Terhune,
Frances Langford, and Phil Regan in *The Hit Parade*.

Charles Kemper
1900-1950

Charles Kemper was born on September 6, 1900, in Oklahoma. He was a veteran of World War I and first appeared on the stage in a show staged by the Thirty-Fifth Division of which he was a member. When he returned to the United States he joined a minstrel show. He later headlined in vaudeville and then joined the George White musicals. He also performed in night clubs and radio. Kemper began his screen career in 1943; he specialized in Western films.

He died in Burbank, California May 12, 1950 as a result of injuries received in an automobile accident. He was a past president of the exclusive Masquers Club. His films included: *The Southerner; Scarlet Street; The Shocking Miss Pilgrim; Gunfighters; Fury at Furnace Creek; Yellow Sky; The Doolins of Oklahoma; Wagonmaster; A Ticket to Tomahawk;* and *The Nevadan.*

Claude King in *Kiss of Araby*.

Charles Kemper, right, with Zachary Scott in *The Southerner*.

British Artillery during World War I. He was born January 15, 1875 in Northampton, England and became an actor there. He came to the United States in 1919 when he appeared in *Declassee*. He started his film career in 1920. In 1935, King, Robert Montgomery, and several others were appointed by the NRA to formulate a code between film players and producers.

He died in Hollywood, September 18, 1941. His films included: *Mysterious Dr. Fu Manchu; Transatlantic; Arrowsmith; Behind the Mask; White Woman; Two Heads on a Pillow; Smart Girl; Shanghai Gesture; Within the Law; New Moon;* and *Kiss of Araby.*

Claude King
1875-1941

Claude King was a retired Major in the British Army. He served two years in France with the

Werner Klemperer (65) 1979

Werner Klemperer, son of the famed symphony

conductor, Otto Klemperer, though having appeared in a number of films is best known as the bumbling Nazi officer, Colonel Klink, on the CBS television series, "Hogan's Heroes."

Although he has a hatred of war and violence, few can equal him at playing a foreign villain. Something of a specialist in unsympathetic roles, Klemperer has a great desire to play an Oriental villain. He believes villainy has a great future in the theatre.

After fleeing Germany in 1933, he ended up in California. He appeared headed for a career as a pianist but gave it up. He went into the theatre after wartime work with the United States Army Special Services. Earning a living as an usher, waiter, and art gallery guide, he finally landed Broadway roles with Tallulah Bankhead, Jose Ferrer; and Charles Laughton. Urbane and sophisticated, he has gone on to carve out a niche in films and television.

His films include: *Ship of Fools*; *Dark Intruder*; *Flight to Hong Kong*; *Istanbul*; *Kiss Them for Me*; *Houseboat*; *Judgement at Nuremberg*; *Escape from East Berlin*; and *Youngblood Hawke*.

Fred Kohler Sr.
1889-1938

Fred Kohler Sr. was born April 20, 1889 in Kansas City, Missouri, the son of an inventor. After his schooling he began his stage career as a spear carrier in his hometown. He then played stock,

Werner Klemperer, center, with Zsa Zsa Gabor and George Sanders in *Death of a Scoundrel*.

116

vaudeville, tent shows, and one night stands. He entered films in 1910 at the old Selig studios and remained in Hollywood and films until his death October 28, 1938.

He virtually always played the "heavy" and was one of the finest. He was at his best in western films and menaced nearly every western hero of the day. His son, Fred Kohler Jr., also became a western badman.

His films included: *Light of the Western Stars; Fighting Caravans; Fiddlin' Buckaroo; Wilderness Mail; Mississippi; Goin' to Town; The Frisco Kid; The Buccaneer;* and *Blockade.*

Alma Kruger.

Fred Kohler.

Alma Kruger
1871-1960

Alma Kruger gained her greatest screen fame in the Dr. Kildare series for M-G-M as the tough nurse, Molly Byrd, who would not bend to anyone, including Lionel Barrymore, who played Dr. Leonard Gillespie in the series. She was born in Pittsburgh and attended Curry University and the American Academy of Dramatic Art. She was prominent in the Shakespearean theatre, then toured nationally. She returned to Broadway to become a permanent member of Eva LeGallienne's Civic Repertory Company. She was heard on radio in "The Goldbergs" and "Those We Love." She died in Seattle, April 5, 1960.

Some of her many films included: *Craig's Wife; Marie Antoinette; The Great Waltz; The Secret of Dr. Kildare; Calling Dr. Gillespie; Three Men in White; Our Hearts Were Young and Gay; A Scandal in Paris;* and *Forever Amber.*

Henry Kulky
1911-1965

Henry Kulky was born August 11, 1911 in Hastings-On-The-Hudson, New York. While in his teens he turned to boxing. After a few bouts he became a wrestling teacher. In 1939 he went to Argentina and became "Bomber Kulkavich" winning 172 matches, losing three; he became the judo champion of South America. He wrestled all the top wrestlers of the day. In 1946, fellow wrestler Mike Mazurki got him a movie role with James Stewart in *Call Northside 777*. This started a nineteen year acting career and in 1950 he quit wrestling for good.

In addition to films he appeared frequently on television with regular roles in "Life of Riley" for five years and his most famous role as Navy Chief Max Bronsky in "Hennessey" starring Jackie Cooper. While studying the script for his role as "Curley" in television's "Voyage to the Bottom of the Sea" he died of a heart attack on February 12, 1965.

Kulky took great pride in the fact he never took an acting lesson. He liked to relate that he learned enough emoting during his seven thousand wrestling matches. His film roles included: *A Likely Story*; *Tarzan's Magic Fountain*; *Bodyhold*; *Love Nest*; *The Glory Brigade*; *The Steel Cage*; *Illegal*; *Up Periscope*; *Guns of the Timberland*; and *A Global Affair*.

Henry Kulky.

John Larkin
1912-1965

Larkin was born in Oakland, California, and moved to Kansas City with his parents at the age of ten. He was graduated from Rockhurst High School and attended Rockhurst College for two years.

Larkin began acting while at Rockhurst College and got his start on local radio stations as an announcer. He broke into network radio in Chicago in 1937 playing soap-opera roles. He served in the signal corps in Europe in World War II and lived in New York after the war.

Familiar to moviegoers and television viewers alike, he also played the lead in several radio shows, including "Perry Mason" and "High Adventure." He was Mike Karr in the daytime television series, "Edge of Night." His appearances in many motion pictures in character roles included: *Saints and Sinners*; *Twelve O'Clock High*; *The Detective*; *Seven Days in May*; *Those Calloways*; and *The Satan Bug*.

Jack LaRue
1902-

Jack LaRue was probably the busiest hood of all when gangster films ruled the screen in the 1930s. Whenever a dope fiend, smuggler, or hired assas-

John Larkin, left, with Linda Evans and Ed Wynn in *Those Calloways*.

Jack LaRue, left, with Phyliss Brooks in *Dangerous Passage*.

sin was needed, he was usually cast in the role. He has made more then two hundred motion pictures in which he was cast as a villain most of the time. Because of his Italian-American ancestry, he was also cast as a priest on numerous occasions. One of his famous roles was that of "Trigger" in 1933 in *The Story of Temple Drake* based on William Faulkner's *Sanctuary*. His other films include: *The Woman Accused; The Mouthpiece; Take the Stand; A Farewell to Arms; Captains Courageous;* and *Slaughter on Tenth Avenue.* LaRue also spent a year and a half making love to Mae West in her Broadway show, *Diamond Lil.*

LaRue devotes his time to his restaurant. To relax he goes to the races. He does not miss the movies too much. "The stuff shot these days is nothing like those old gangster classics. Villains today? It's a lost art."

Lucille Laverne
1872-1945

Lucille Laverne was at her best playing repulsive old hags as she did in D.W. Griffith's *Orphans of the Storm* in 1921 or in *Tale of Two Cities* released by M-G-M in 1935. She was born in Nashville, Tennessee on November 8, 1872. She started her career as a child actress and made her first New York stage appearance in 1888. In 1895 she went on tour of the United States with her own company and played command performances before the crowned heads of Europe. She continued in legitimate theater and made her first film in 1914. Her motion picture career ended when she played the voice of the queen and the wicked witch for

Lucille LaVerne, standing right, with Fritz Leiber, Barlowe Borland, Blanche Yurka, and Mitchell Lewis in *A Tale of Two Cities*.

Ivan Lebedeff, left, with Gloria Roy in *Fair Warning*.

Disney's classic, *Snow White and the Seven Dwarfs*. She retired and became a co-owner of a night club. She died March 4, 1945.

Among her film credits were: *Abraham Lincoln; Little Caesar; An American Tragedy; Alias the Doctor; Hearts of Humanity; Wild Horse Mesa; Strange Adventure; Pilgrimage; Beloved;* and *Kentucky Kernels*.

Ivan Lebedeff
1894-1953

Ivan Lebedeff played roles that required an ur-bane man of the world that you wouldn't want to trust with your wife. He was born June 18, 1894 in Uspoliai, Lithuania and attended the college of St. Petersburg in St. Petersburg, Russia before he made his film debut in a German film in 1922 called *King Frederick*. He appeared in several French films and was brought to the United States to play in D. W. Griffith's *The Sorrows of Satan* released in 1926. This started a long screen career in America. Lebedeff also wrote several screen plays, had one script accepted by Frank Capra, and authored a novel in 1940 called *Legion of Dishonor.* He was married to actress Vera Engels. He died March 31, 1953 in Hollywood.

Some of his films included: *Midnight Mystery; Deceit; Bombshell; Merry Widow; China Seas; Love on the Run; Conquest; You Can't Cheat an Honest Man; Passport to Alcatraz; Shanghai Gesture;* and *Mission to Moscow.*

George J. Lewis
1903-

George Joseph Lewis was born December 10, 1903 in Guadalajara, Mexico and attended high school in San Diego before beginning his film career in 1923 as an extra. He was groomed for stardom by Universal and in 1925 had the lead in *His People.* He gradually drifted into character parts and in addition to many featured films appeared in many serials in the 1940s. He also appeared on the stage, radio, and television. As he grew older he was ideal for any role that required a sense of Spanish dignity such as his role in Disney's "Zorro" for television for three years starting in 1957. He played Zorro's father. Lewis was also a close friend of Alan Ladd and played in many of his films before retiring in 1962 and began to devote full time to his successful real estate business.

His films include: *Lazy River; Captain Calamity; Back Door to Heaven; The Falcon in Mexico; Wagon Wheels Westward; Appointment with Danger; Desert Legion; Shane; Santiago;* and *The Comancheros.*

George J. Lewis, right, with Joe Sawyer and Glenn Ford in *Gilda*.

Doris Lloyd
?-1968

Doris Lloyd was born in Liverpool, England, and appeared on the British stage before migrating to the United States in 1924. For many years she appeared in featured roles on the screen. She appeared in Los Angeles on the stage in the 1920s in such plays as: *The Fog; Secrets;* and *Spring Cleaning.*

Her last film was *Sound of Music.* Included in her long list of film credits are: *Journey for Margaret; Ghost of Frankenstein; The Lodger; My Name Is Julia Ross; Devotion; The Conspirators; Three Strangers; Molly and Me; Scotland Yard Investigation;* and *Escape Me Never.*

James Lydon
1923-

Jimmy Lydon has been a professional for more than forty years. Born in Harrington Park, N.J., of nontheatrical parents, Lydon was part of the last of a vital Broadway stage—the best of the film era and the onslaught of live and film television.

A John Robert Powers child at age eight, Lydon has had a busy career ever since. By ten he was embarked on a radio career and at fourteen was launched upon a Broadway career. Then at sixteen he went to Hollywood and into films at RKO, Paramount, Warners, and Columbia. With the advent of television he appeared on both live and filmed television series, plus guest shots on most leading shows.

Lydon was to experience two major handicaps in his career. One was typecasting (squeaky-voiced, typical American high schooler) and the other, never publicized: he was born with clubfeet. Neither handicap has stopped him.

Today, Lydon is a busy executive behind the cameras at 20th Century Fox on the production end of the business. Producer or actor, the fact remains, it was Henry Aldrich that made Lydon a star and it is as Henry that he will be remembered by most movie fans.

Doris Lloyd, left, with Ida Lupino and Gig Young in *Escape Me Never*.

Flying, hunting, and being an amateur chef are his hobbies. Married and with two daughters, Jimmy Lydon considers his best memories in show business to be those of the people he worked with, "wonderful people such as actor Robert Armstrong, Frank McHugh, Alan Ladd, Ernest Truex, Elizabeth Taylor, and Jimmy Cagney—so many fascinating, talented people."

His many film credits include: *Tom Brown's School Days*—his favorite role; *The Time of Your Life*; *Little Men*; *Two Thoroughbreds*; *Henry Aldrich* series; *Gasoline Alley*; *Corky of Gasoline Alley*; *The Hypnotic Eye*; *Brainstorm*; *Death of a Gunfighter*; plus so many other films.

James Lydon, right, with Lois Collier in *Out of the Storm*.

William H. Lynn
1888-1952

William H. Lynn was a native of Providence, Rhode Island. He was graduated from Brown University where he was president of the dramatic club. He started on the stage where he was a singer and dancer in *The Spring Chicken;* later he was in vaudeville, stock, and with various touring companies. Lynn was a spritely, kindly old gentleman and played the little fellow with the gift of picking winners in *Three Men on a Horse* for its Broadway run of five hundred performances during 1935 and 1936. In films he had two particularly good roles as "Judge Gaffney" in *Harvey* starring James Stewart in 1950 for Universal, and in 1951 he was one of the old folks (Mr. Beebe) in Clifton Webb's *Mr. Belve-*

dere Rings the Bell. Other films were: *Katie Did It; The Outcasts of Poker Flat;* and *The Twonky.* He died January 5, 1952 in New York of a heart ailment.

Mercedes McCambridge
1918-

Miss McCambridge was born in Joliet, Illinois. Much of her childhood was spent on the family farm in Blackstone, Illinois.

She received a B.A. degree from Mundelein College in Chicago. Her first acting experience occurred here in Shakespeare. While in college, she signed a contract with NBC for broadcasting out of

William Lynn, left, with Clifton Webb in *Mr. Belvedere Rings the Bell*.

Mercedes McCambridge.

Chicago. Shortly afterward, she became radio's busiest actress and according to Orson Welles, "the world's greatest living radio actress." She appeared on hundreds of radio programs playing among others, *Big Sister* and *Nora Drake* of the soap operas.

Miss McCambridge's first stage role was in *Hope for the Best*. She also appeared in *A Place of our Own; Twilight Bar;* and *Woman Bites Dog.*

Mercedes McCambridge had the distinction of winning an Academy Award for her first film, *All the King's Men.* Since her debut in this film, she has appeared in such films as: *Lightning Strikes Twice; Inside Straight; The Scarf; Johnny Guitar;* and *Giant.*

A person of great warmth, Miss McCambridge doesn't like to dress up and never shops for clothes. She wore a thirteen-year-old evening dress to the Academy Award ceremonies. Miss McCambridge calls it her career dress because so many good things have happened to her while wearing it. She paid fifty-five dollars for the dress in Chicago in 1937. Recently, she had an unbilled role as the voice of the demon in *The Exorcist.*

Kenneth MacDonald.

Kenneth MacDonald
1901-1972

Kenneth MacDonald was born Kenneth Dollins in Portland, Indiana. He was an outstanding athlete in high school and also possessed a fine singing voice. In the 1920s he began appearing on the American stage in all of the major cities. MacDonald arrived on the Hollywood scene in the early 1930s and quickly landed bit roles in films. He wasn't getting anywhere so he prepared a booklet entitled *The Case of Kenneth MacDonald* and distributed it to the motion picture industry in 1933. In effect, it said "Here I am, I'm available." It worked! A versatile actor, he appeared in many types of roles, but western fans will particularly remember him for the Charles Starrett westerns (Columbia) in the late thirties and early forties. He was a frequent visitor into the homes of television viewers as he played the judge in sixty episodes of the "Perry Mason" television series as well as many other shows.

His films included: *Spoilers of the Range, Island of Doomed Men; The Durango Kid; Confessions of Boston Blackie; First Yank into Tokyo; Hellfire; Sugarfoot; The Caine Mutiny; The Ten Commandments; The Family Band;* and *Which Way to the Front.*

Wilbur Mack
1873-1964

Wilbur Mack was born July 29, 1873 in Binghamton, New York. He started his career as a blackface comedian, then became a featured player in a repertory company at the age of nineteen. He organized, managed, and acted in his own dramatic stock company, with which he toured for four years. Mack and his wife (who later became screen actress Nella Walker) played the major circuits

Wilbur Mack, in business suit, with Bud McClure, John Wayne, Raymond Hatton, and Cactus Mack in *New Frontier*.

under the name of "Mack and Walker." When talkies started, he followed many of the other vaudeville performers and started in films in 1928 and remained active until 1959. Mack became one of the oldest screen extras appearing in films as he still took an occasional role after his retirement. At the age of ninety he was still playing golf and remained a dapper dresser which was one of his trademarks. He died in Hollywood, March 13, 1964.

Some of his pictures were: *Slim Fingers; The Argyle Case; Czar of Broadway; Up the River; Redheads on Parade; Larceny on the Air; Law of the Texan; Half a Sinner; Dixie; Atlantic City;* and *Stage Struck.*

Mala
1906-1952

Ray Mala was born near Candle, Alaska in 1906. His father was an American trader and his mother was an Eskimo. He attended the Kotzbue Territorial school and as a youth he traveled extensively, hunting and fishing in the North American Arctic regions. Mack made his screen debut in *Igloo* for Universal in 1932 and two years later starred in *Eskimo* for M-G-M. He was known simply as Mala in his films. In 1936 he was chosen to star in Republic's fourteen chapter serial *Robinson*

Mala in *The Jungle Princess*.

Crusoe of Clipper Island and followed this in 1938 as a co-star with Bruce Bennett in the same studio's twelve chapter serial, *Hawk of the Wilderness*.

Other feature films that he appeared in were: *The Last of the Pagans; Call of the Yukon; Mutiny on the Blackhawk; Green Hell; Zanzibar; The Devil's Pipeline; Girl from God's Country; The Tuttles of Tahiti;* and *The Girl from Alaska*. He also worked as an assistant cameraman between films. He died of a heart attack September 23, 1952.

Hank Mann
1887-1971

Hank Mann was the last survivor of Mack Sennett's original Keystone Kops. He entered motion pictures in 1912 and played one of the bumbling, bowler-hatted policemen in numerous movies. Mann remained with Sennett after the passing of

Hank Mann, right, with Chester Lauck and Norris Goff in *Two Weeks to Live*.

the Kops, then starred in his own series of comedies before switching to feature films which included such films as: *Modern Times; Smokey; The Garden of Eden;* and *Hollywood Cavalcade.* In 1943, when acting assignments became scarce, Mann became a makeup man for such stars as Edward Everett Horton and Ernest Truex. Mann later opened a small malt shop in Sierra Madre, California, and made occasional character appearances in films as late as 1960. He died in a convalescent hospital in South Pasadena on November 25, 1971, only six weeks after the death of Chester Conklin, another of the Kops. Other films in which Mann appeared included: *The Arizona Kid; City Lights; Million Dollar Legs; Down Trail; The Great Dictator; Man of a Thousand Faces;* and *Two Weeks to Live.*

George Marion
1860-1945

George Marion was born in San Francisco July 16, 1860. He received his stage training there and played for stock companies. Marion was with Lew Dockstader's Minstrels in 1888 and became a director for Florenz Ziegfeld beginning in 1896, directing such stars as Anna Held, Will Rogers, and Fanny Brice. He was happy in this capacity until 1919 when he played "Toby," an old Negro servant in *Toby's Bow.* Marion directed revivals of many plays for the Shuberts from 1920 to 1929. He gained his greatest fame playing the old sea captain, "Chris Christopherson" in *Anna Christie* first on the stage in 1921, then in the silent screen version in 1923, and finally the sound effort in 1939 with Greta Garbo for M-G-M. Marion died in Carmel, California on November 30, 1945.

Among his films were: *The Bishop Murder Case: The Sea Bat; The Big House; Pay Off; A Lady's Morals; Should Kiss; Man to Man; Hook Line and Sinker; Six Hours to Live; Her First Mate;* and *Port of Lost Dreams.*

George Marion, left, with Greta Garbo in *Anna Christie*.

John Marley.

John Marley

Born in Harlem of immigrant Russian parents, Marley learned his craft by watching, observing, and working in acting groups in and around New York.

He made his first film in 1942, *Native Land*, and was then drafted into the United States Army. While in the service he did three shows a week visiting overseas areas. After the war, Marley did network shows for ABC and later directed summer stock, regional theatre and for universities.

His recent films include: *Cat Ballou*; *America, America*; *Love Story* (He played Phil Caverieri for which he was nominated for an Oscar and Golden Globe); *Faces* (Best Actor award, Venice Film Festival); and *The Godfather*. Marley has also done much television work.

An avid tennis player, Marley has refused many acting offers because it interfered with his game.

Tully Marshall
1864-1943

Tully Marshall was born William Phillips in Nevada City, California on April 13, 1864. He intended to pursue a legal career until he ventured into a dramatic course at Santa Clara University.

Tully Marshall, left, with Jean Harlow in *Red Dust*.

He started his stage work in San Francisco in 1883. In 1887 he moved to New York City and played in a variety of roles on Broadway and on the road. After a few minor roles in films he was given the opportunity to play the High Priest of Babylon in the film classic, *Intolerance*, released in 1916. His finest role in silent films was playing an old frontiersman in *The Covered Wagon* in 1923. When talkies arrived he was still very much in demand as he worked for nearly every major studio. His last film was *Behind Prison Walls* in 1943. He died March 10, 1943 after an acting career of sixty years. His films included: *The Big Trail; Scarface; Grand Hotel; Red Dust; Massacre; A Tale of Two Cities; Chad Hanna; This Gun for Hire;* and *Gentlemen from West Point.*

Marion Martin
1916-

Marion Martin was one of those tough, wise-cracking broads that graced the screen in the 1930s and 1940s. She was of the same mold as Veda Ann Borg, Iris Adrian, and Barbara Pepper. She was born June 7, 1916 in Philadelphia, the daughter of a stage actress, and attended Bayonne School in Switzerland. She made her stage debut in the *Follies of 1933* and then *George White's Scandals.* She was supposedly the last girl that Ziegfeld glorified before his death. She was once described as the most gorgeous girl on Broadway. She made

Marion Martin, left, with Harpo Marx in *The Big Store*.

her film debut in *Sinners in Paradise* in 1938. She retired from films in 1950. Other films that the platinum blonde appeared in were: *Boom Town; The Big Store; Lady Scarface; Mexican Spitfire at Sea; The Lady of Burlesque; Irish Eyes Are Smiling; It Happened Tomorrow; Cinderella Jones; Come to the Stable;* and *Key to the City.*

Strother Martin
1919- 1982

During the past twenty years it was a sure bet that if a director needed a slightly neurotic villain they would call on Strother Martin. He was born March 26, 1919 in Kokomo, Indiana and was graduated from high school in Indianapolis. During World War II he joined the United States Navy and was commissioned. He studied to be an actor at the University of Michigan and while there he was a champion diver and nearly made the Olympic squad. He came to Hollywood in 1948 and only managed to do little theatre, but later he got a few small parts on television including "Gunsmoke." His first film appearance was a small, non-speaking role in *Asphalt Jungle* in 1950. He appeared in many films thereafter, but his career really didn't blossom until he played the captain of a prison farm in *Cool Hand Luke* in 1967. Martin is adept at comedy as proven in his role as "Colonel Stonehill" in *True Grit* in 1969. He gained audience sympathy in *Fool's Parade* with James Stewart and was completely without conscience as a killer teamed with Jack Elam and Ernest Borgnine in *Hannie Caulder* in 1972. His other films include:

Strother Martin, right, with George C. Scott in *The Flim-Flam Man*.

133

Paul Maxey, left, with Pat O'Brien and George Raft in *A Dangerous Profession*.

Strategic Air Command; Copper Sky; McLintock!; Shenandoah; The Flim-Flam Man; The Wild Bunch; Butch Cassidy and the Sundance Kid; Ballad of Cable Hogue; and *Red Sky at Morning.*

Paul Maxey
1907-1963

Paul Maxey was a rotund actor who was very active in films, television, and stage productions. He was Mr. Peoples on "Peoples Choice" on tele-vision for several years. He also appeared on "Lassie"; "Dennis the Menace"; and the "Joey Bishop Show." He was very active in productions at the Pasadena Playhouse, appearing in 187 plays. He was born March 15, 1907 in Wheaton, Illinois and moved to Pasadena in 1923. He was a member of the Advisory Committee of Actors Equity. He died of a heart attack in Pasadena June 3, 1963. Among his film credits were: *Below the Deadline; Millie's Daughter; Philo Vance's Secret Mission; Bride for Sale; Joe Palooka in the Big Fight; Sky Dragon; Curtain Call at Cactus Creek; Casa Mañana; The Narrow Margin; Here Comes the Marines;* and *A Dangerous Profession.*

Myron McCormick
1908-1962

Myron McCormick was an actor's actor. Although adept at comedy, he was also a fine dramatic actor. He had prominent roles in two Broadway smash hits; in *South Pacific* he played the free-wheeling Seabee Luther Billis and Sergeant King in *No Time for Sergeants*. He won the coveted Donaldson Award in 1949 for his role in *South Pacific*. He was born February 8, 1908 in Albany Indiana. When he was only eleven he was already touring with a medicine show. McCormick attended New Mexico Military Institute and later went to Princeton where he graduated in 1931. He was on Broadway a year later. During the golden era of radio McCormick was always in demand. His parts ranged from soap operas such as "Portia Faces Life" and "Joyce Jordan, Girl Interne" to dramas such as "Mr. District Attorney"; "Gang Busters"; and "Inner Sanctum." He repeated his role as Sergeant King in *No Time for Sergeants* in

Myron McCormick in *No Time for Sergeants*.

1958 for Warner Bros. and also appeared in such films as *Jigsaw; Jolson Sings Again; Not as a Stranger; Three for the Show; The Man Who Understood Women;* and his last; *The Hustler*. He died in New York of cancer July 30, 1962.

George McKay
1885-1945

George McKay was born April 15, 1884 in Minsk, Russia. He was raised in a Cleveland Jewish orphan home. Although the family name was Reuben he changed his name to McKay when he left the home. He got his start in show business as a singing waiter in Chicago. He also became a bareback rider and clown with the Harris Nickel Plate Circus. McKay traveled with tent shows and later worked in the Gus Edwards musical *Merry-Go-Round* and in the musical *Honey Girl*. He was in the Ziegfeld Follies of 1913, 1914, and 1915, and he was in vaudeville for a number of years with Johnny Cantwell under the name of McKay and Cantwell. He then worked with his wife Ottine Ardine. They were featured for many years on the Keith and Orpheum circuits and in Europe. He was one of the founders of the National Vaudeville Artists. McKay was signed as a contract player for Columbia and appeared in the following films: *Killer at Large; Counterfeit Lady; It's All Yours; There's Always a Woman; Convicted; King of the Turf; Behind Prison Gates; Pardon My Stripes; Sweetheart of the Fleet; The Boogie Man Will Get You;* and *Louisiana Hayride*. He died December 3, 1945 in Hollywood.

Edward McNamara
1887-1944

Edward McNamara was born in Paterson, New Jersey. He became a policeman in that city, but he had a voice with lots of promise and was sent to the School of Music at the University of Michigan by

George McKay, left, with Richard Dix in *Submarine*.

Madame Schumann-Heink. McNamara was also coached by the great Enrico Caruso. He entered show business as an Irish tenor and later went into legitimate acting. Because of his Irish brogue and robust stature he was often typed for cop roles on Broadway and in motion pictures. He created the role of a cop in *Strictly Dishonorable* on the stage. On November 10, 1944 he was traveling in an express car talking to his longtime friend, James Cagney when he was stricken with a fatal heart attack. Among his films were: *I Am a Fugitive from a Chain Gang*; *Silver Dollar*; *20,000 Years in Sing Sing*; *Great Guy*; *Girl Overboard*; *The League of Frightened Men*; *The Devil and Miss Jones*; *Strawberry Blonde*; *Margin for Error*; *Johnny Come Lately*; and his last film *Arsenic and Old Lace*, he played Brophy, the cop.

Howard McNear
1905-1969

Best known for his pencil mustache, voice inflection and comedy, Howard McNear was in show business forty-four years. He is probably best remembered for his television role of Floyd, the barber, on the "Andy Griffith" television show, a jittery character who didn't finish sentences.

McNear, though known for comedy, was equally adept at straight roles. He portrayed the Doc Adams character on "Gunsmoke" when the series first appeared on radio. On television he played opposite George Burns and Gracie Allen, George Gobel, Jack Benny, and others.

136

**Edward McNamara, left, with Raymond Massey and Jack
Carson in *Arsenic and Old Lace*.**

**Howard McNear, right, with June Allyson and Elvia Allman
in *You Can't Run Away from It*.**

Butterfly McQueen in *Duel in the Sun*.

In demand for character roles in Hollywood, McNear's numerous feature films included: *The Errand Boy*; *Irma LaDouce*; *Bell, Book, and Candle*; *The Big Circus*; *Anatomy of a Murder*; and *You Can't Run Away from It*.

Patrick McVey, center, with John Carroll and Fredrick K. Worlock in *Pierre of the Plains*.

Butterfly McQueen
1911-

Miss McQueen made her film debut in what was to become her most famous role, that of Prissy in *Gone with the Wind*. Miss McQueen was twenty-nine when the movie was made. Her role called for her to portray Prissy as a girl of thirteen.

Despite good reviews for her performance, good roles were rare and Miss McQueen's Hollywood career never rose above the level of the "stereotype Negro." When this type of role gave out in the late 1940s, she returned to the stage, where the parts turned out to be no better. There were occasional parts on television (Oreole on the "Beulah" series) and then lean years as a factory worker, waitress, and dishwasher.

In recent years the picture has brightened with Miss McQueen's return to the stage in New York in *Curly McDimple* and the growing dinner theatre movement in the United States.

Her film credits include: *The Women*; *Mildred Pierce*; *Cabin in the Sky*; *Since You Went Away*; and *Duel in the Sun*. Regarding the new black films, Miss McQueen enjoyed *The Learning Tree* but has avoided the others because of "vulgar language." As for future roles she said: "I'd like to play just an American, they can see I'm black."

Patrick McVey
1910-1973

Patrick McVey, a graduate of Indiana University in 1931 and later from its law school, switched from law to acting. In 1938 he joined the Pasadena Playhouse and thus began a successful career as a character actor in the theatre, films, and television.

On television, McVey had played Steve Wilson in "Big Town" and also acted in "Boots and Saddles" and "Manhunt." His Broadway appearances included: *Crime and Punishment*; *Detective Story*; *Bus Stop*; and *The Subject Was Roses*.

His film career, which spanned a number of years, included *Party Girl*; *North by Northwest*; and *The Visitors*.

He was a member of the Actors Studio and The Players.

Edward McWade
1864-1943

Edward McWade was the older brother of the famed character actor Robert McWade. He was born on January 14, 1865 in Washington, D.C. Before coming to Hollywood in 1923 he played the Eastern Vaudeville circuits for twenty-five years. During the silents he was a screen writer and later took up acting. While working on his part as "Mr. Gibbs" for *Arsenic and Old Lace* he became ill and died May 16, 1943. His films included: *Big Shot*; *Murders in the Zoo*; *Notorious Sophie Lang*; *Oil for the Lamps of China*; *Dr. Socrates*; *Reunion*; *They*

Edward McWade, left, with Georgia Caine, Josephine Hull and Cary Grant in *Arsenic and Old Lace*.

Won't Forget; Garden of the Moon; Indianapolis Speedway; The Return of Frank James; and *Nothing But the Truth.*

Robert McWade
1872-1938

Robert McWade was known as the "loveable grouch" of films. Both his father and grandfather were stage actors, he simply followed in their foot- steps. He was born on June 17, 1872 in Buffalo, New York and began his stage career in 1902 with the Murray Hill stock company and later became a Broadway star appearing in the original *Ben Hur.* McWade came to Hollywood in 1925 to appear on the stage and soon switched to films. His brother, Edward McWade, was also a film character actor. McWade had just finished his role in *Of Human Hearts* starring James Stewart and was still on the set when he died January 19, 1938. His films included: *Grand Hotel; Back Street; 42nd Street; Kennel Murder Case; Lemon Drop Kid; The President Vanishes; County Chairman; His Night Out; Anything Goes; Good Old Soak;* and *Gold Is Where You Find It.*

Robert McWade in *Flaming Gold*.

Adolphe Menjou
1890-1963

White spats, an ascot tie, a walking stick, and a trimmed moustache, when they were put all together they became the debonair actor, Adolphe Menjou. His name consistently appeared on the nation's ten best dressed men. He once boasted his wardrobe consisted of two thousand articles including one hundred suits. He was born in Pittsburgh, February 18, 1890 where his father was in the hotel and restaurant business. He attended Culver Military Academy, then Cornell University. In his third year, he left school to join his father in the restaurant business in Cleveland. He then went to New York. After several jobs he was an extra in *The Man behind the Door* as a ringmaster. He soon became a regular extra usually as a villain. When World War I came along he enlisted in an ambulance unit, served in France and was discharged as a captain. After the war, he went to Hollywood and played minor roles until 1923 when better parts came his way. In 1930 he played the hard-boiled editor in *The Front Page* and was nominated for his only Academy Award. He played many types of roles including a motion-picture producer, a trial lawyer, a floor walker or an unscrupulous villain. During World War II he made broadcasts in French, Italian, Spanish, German, and Russian for the Office of War Information. In 1948 he wrote his autobiography entitled *It Took Nine Tailors*. He was a staunch anti-Communist and testified in the sensational trials of 1947. In his later years he was more interested in Republican affairs than in acting. His films included: *Morocco; Morning Glory; Little Miss Marker; A Star Is Born; Stage Door; Roxie Hart; State of the Union; Across the Wide Missouri; The Sniper; Man on a Tightrope; Paths of Glory;* and *Pollyanna*. He was also the host for "My Favorite Story" on television. He died of chronic hepatitis in Beverly Hills on October 29, 1963.

Adolphe Menjou, left, with Charlie Ruggles in *Wives Never Know*.

Beryl Mercer, right, with Robert Montgomery in *Night Must Fall*.

Beryl Mercer
1862-1939

Beryl Mercer became, on film, the symbol of respectable motherhood. She added dignity to any role she played. She was born in Seville, Spain on August 13, 1862, the daughter of a Spanish diplomat. Her mother was Beryl Montague, a leading lady of the stage. She first appeared on the stage at the age of four. When Beryl Mercer was ten she definitely decided on acting as a career, and for the next five years she became the most popular impersonator of boy's roles in London. She made her American debut in 1906 at the Lyric Theatre in *The Schulamite* and made her screen debut in 1922 in *The Christian*. One of her best-known roles was that of "Mrs. Midget" in *Outward Bound* on Broadway in 1924. The role was recreated on film in 1930. By the time she was fifty she was one of the delightful young-old ladies on the screen. Her first talkie was *Mother's Boy* for Pathé and other films included: *Three Live Ghosts; All Quiet on the Western Front; Public Enemy; Cavalcade; Jane Eyre; Magnificent Obsession; Call It A Day; Night Must Fall;* and *Hound of the Baskervilles.* After having undergone major surgery, she died July 28, 1939.

Charles Meredith, left, with Robert Armstrong in *The Streets of San Francisco*.

Charles Meredith
1894-1964

Charles Meredith was a leading man in silent films reaching his peak from 1919 through 1923. He starred in such films as *Luck in Pawn* with Marguerite Clark in 1919; *Simple Souls* with Blanche Sweet in 1920; and *The Beautiful Liar* with Katherine MacDonald in 1921. He was born August 27, 1894 in Pennsylvania and was on Broadway and the eastern stage. Meredith gracefully entered character parts as he got older and was adept at playing military officers, ministers, businessmen, and similar roles. He also made many television appearances, his last being "The Seven Little Foys." He died in Hollywood November 28, 1964. His films included: *Daisy Kenyon*; *The Boy with Green Hair*; *Tokyo Joe*; *Perfect Strangers*; *The Sun Sets at Dawn: Al Jennings of Oklahoma*; *The Big Trees*; *Cattle Town*; *Chicago Confidential*; *The Buccaneer*; and *Twelve Hours to Kill*.

Philip Merivale
1886-1946

Philip Merivale was born in Rehutia, India on November 2, 1886. When he was a youngster he went to London and attended Oxford. He gave up his education for the stage in 1905 and became one of the foremost Shakespearean actors. He came to the United States in 1914 with Mrs. Patrick Campbell to appear in *Pygmalion*. Merivale served in the Canadian Air Force during World War I and upon his return resumed his career. His best role on Broadway was in 1929 in *Death Takes a Holiday* but his personal favorite role was that of Hannibal in *The Road to Rome*. In 1935, Gladys Cooper and Merivale produced *Othello* and *MacBeth* and in 1937 he married the famous actress. His film career began in 1932. Some of his films were: *Give Us the Night; Mr. and Mrs. Smith; Midnight Angel; Lady for a Night; This Above All; Crossroads; This Land Is Mine; The Hour before Dawn; Tonight and Every Night;* and *Adventure*. Several times he was voted as one of the ten handsomest men in the United States. He died March 13, 1946.

Philip Merivale, left, with Orson Welles, Loretta Young, and Byron Keith in *The Stranger*.

Robert Middlemass
1885-1949

Robert Middlemass appeared as a character actor in many films in the 1930s and 1940s, but he is known best as the author of *The Valiant*, a famous one-act play. He was born September 3, 1885 in New Britain, Connecticut. Middlemass attended Harvard working his way through college as a hotel headwaiter. Even though he always wanted to become an actor, he studied playwrighting in college. He was a member of the Castle Square stock company in Boston and played in stock throughout America. He wrote many plays including *Budget*; *The Handy Man*; *Americans All*; and *The Clutching Claw*. For diversion when he was not writing or acting he became an expert magician. His films included: *Air Fury*; *The Lone Wolf Returns*; *Cain and Mabel*; *A Day at the Races*; *Navy Blue and Gold*; *Spawn of the North*; *Kentucky*; *Stanley and Livingston*; *Little Old New York*; *Wilson*; and *The Dolly Sisters*.

Robert Middlemass, right, with Randolph Scott in *Coast Guard*.

Silvio Minciotti, left, with Esther Minciotti, Janet Leigh, and Ezio Pinza in *Strictly Dishonorable*.

Silvio Minciotti
1882-1961

Silvio Minciotti was born in Italy and came to the United States as the youngest member of the Eleanora Duse legitimate company. They toured the United States and Europe. He turned to Broadway and appeared in many productions including *A Bell for Adano* and *Best House in Naples*.

He also appeared in several films. His wife was Esther Minciotti who was so believable as Ernest Borgnine's mother in *Marty* (1955). They were in many plays and films together and were known as the Barrymores of the Italian-American stage. He died May 2, 1961 in Elmhurst, New York. His films included: *Deported; Up Front; Strictly Dishonorable; Clash by Night; Francis Covers the Big Town; Kiss Me Deadly; Serenade; Full of Life;* and *Wives Never Know*.

George Mitchell
1905-1972

George Mitchell usually appeared as a villain, and in recent years was seen frequently in numerous television westerns including "Have Gun, Will Travel"; "Bonanza"; "The Virginian"; and "Gunsmoke." He was born in Larchmont, New York, on February 21, 1905. It was not until he was thirty-five , and newly married to actress Katherine Squire, that he decided to be an actor. A veteran of stage, films, and television, he died in his sleep on January 18, 1972, in Washington, D.C. where Mitchell was in rehearsal for the Arena Theatre's *Conflict of Interest*. He had been on Broadway as Chief Joseph in Arthur Kapit's *Indians* and was also the drunken survivor in the film, *The Andromeda Strain*. His other films include: *Twilight of Honor; 3:10 to Yuma; Two-Lane Blacktop; Birdman of Alcatraz; Kid Galahad; The Flim-Flam Man;* and *The Wild and the Innocent*.

George Mitchell in *The Phenix City Story*.

Millard Mitchell
1903-1953

Millard Mitchell was one of the best of the character actors whether it was a straight dramatic role, a hard–boiled cynic or comedy. He came to the screen after appearing in over fifty Broadway plays. Mitchell was born in Havana, Cuba on August 14, 1903. He hated school and quit high school to work at various jobs such as: a cowhand; steward; adjuster; insurance investigator; electrician; and salesman. In 1925 while working as a box-office man he was asked to substitute at rehearsals for a part in a play that was for a man of his size. It was to last only until another actor could be found. Mitchell stayed on to play the role and made his Broadway debut in *The Holy Terror*. Other Broadway plays were: *The Front Page; Blessed Event; Yellow Jack;* and *Kiss the Boys Goodbye*. He made his film bow in *Mr. and Mrs. North* in 1941. His other films included: *The Mayor of 44th Street; Slightly Dangerous; A Foreign Affair; Twelve O'Clock High; The Gunfighter; Winchester 73; Mr.*

Millard Mitchell in *My Six Convicts*.

880; Strictly Dishonorable; My Six Convicts; The Naked Spur; and his last film was *Here Come the Girls!* Mitchell was up for a choice role in *White Christmas;* but was forced to withdraw due to illness. He died October 13, 1953 of cancer.

Mantan Moreland
1902-1973

Born in Monroe, Louisiana, Moreland ran away with a circus at fourteen. Appearing in circuses and carnivals, he later joined a comedy vaudeville act. His first film role was secured through Joe Louis and was in *Spirit of St. Louis.*

Moreland made a total of 310 pictures. His trademarks were his popeyed expression and his line, "Feets, do your stuff." He also specialized in what he called his "indefinite routine, which he performed in the Chan films with the late Benny Carter. One would begin a sentence, the other would interrupt, and the exchanges would lead into mental brick walls.

Moreland was seen in several Frankie Darro films for Monogram before moving into the Chan pictures. He played the chauffeur, Birmingham Brown, in the Charlie Chan movies to all three Chans, Warner Oland, Sidney Toler, and Roland Winters. Moreland worked with comedian Redd Foxx in New York's Apollo Theatre and more recently appeared on such television shows as "Love American Style"; "Adam 12"; and "The Bill Cosby Show." His many film credits include: *Cabin in the Sky* (favorite role); *Biscuit Eater; International Lady; Watermelon Man; King of the Zombies;* and *One Dark Night.* His hobbies were baseball, cards and traveling.

Mantan Moreland.

Frank Morgan
1890-1949

Frank Morgan was born Francis Philip Wuppermann in New York City. After attending Cornell University he worked at different jobs before deciding to join his older brother, Ralph Morgan, in the acting profession. He had a turn in vaudeville on the New York stage, then landed a part as the juvenile lead in *Mr. Wu.* When Earle Williams left Anita Stewart's company he became her leading man. Morgan entered motion pictures for Vitagraph. Morgan was nominated for an Oscar for best supporting actor in *Affairs of Cellini* in 1934, and was nominated for best supporting actor in *Tortilla Flat* in 1942. He can be seen each year on television as "The Wizard" in the film classic *The Wizard of Oz.* He also starred on radio in the "Maxwell House Coffee Time" program which featured Fanny Brice as "Baby Snooks." His films included: *The Cat and the Fiddle; Naughty Marietta; The Great Ziegfeld; The Shop around the Corner; Boomtown; Honky Tonk; The Stratton Story; Any Number Can Play;* and *Key to the City.*

Frank Morgan, left, with Clark Gable in *Honky Tonk*.

"LIFE IS SO, SO, TOO, TOO SHORT!"

Adrian Morris
1907-1941

Adrian Morris was born January 12, 1907 in Mt. Vernon, New York. He was the son of the prominent actor William Morris and his mother was Etta Hawkins, and outstanding comedienne. He appeared on the stage with his family in a vaudeville act that also included his older brother, Chester, who went on to become a motion picture star. Morris came to Hollywood in 1929 and appeared in many films as a character actor. This included many small-time hoodlum or rough-neck roles. He was a sidekick for Grant Withers in two serials, *The Fighting Marines* in 1935 for Mascot and *Radio Patrol* in 1937 for Universal. He was scheduled to appear in one of his brother's films when he died suddenly on November 30, 1941. Some of his films included: *Me and My Gal; Bureau of Missing Persons; Big Shakedown; The G-Men; Dr. Socrates; The Petrified Forest; There Goes the Groom; Angels with Dirty Faces; Return of the Cisco Kid;* and *The Grapes of Wrath.*

Adrian Morris, right, with Warner Baxter in *The Return of the Cisco Kid*.

Maurice Moscovitch
1871-1940

Maurice Moscovitch was born November 23, 1871 in Odessa, Russia. He was chosen by his parents to become a jeweler and a watchmaker. As a small boy he started hanging around the stage door of the National Theatre of Odessa and soon learned the art of moustache dressing and wig making. He received his first role at the age of fourteen and left home when his father disapproved of his new career. In 1893 he came to New York where he made his first appearance at the Windsor Theatre for five dollars a week. Moscovitch became a favorite performer on the Yiddish stage and did not make his English speaking debut until he was forty-eight years of age. He acted in five languages and toured every continent. His films included: *Susannah of the Mounties; Everything Happens at Night; Winterset; The Great Dictator; South to Karanga; Rio; Make Way for Tomorrow; Suez; Love Affair; Lancer Spy; Gateway;* and *In Name Only.* He was working in RKO's *Dance, Girl, Dance* when he died June 18, 1940 leaving his large collection of old violins.

Maurice Moscovich right, with Charles Boyer in *Love Affair*.

Charlie Murray in *The Cohens and Kellys in Africa*.

Charlie Murray
1872-1941

Charlie Murray was born June 22, 1872 in Laurel, Indiana. After a stage career where teamed as Murray and Mack for twenty-one years, he started in pictures with the old Biograph Company in 1912. He made many comedies for Mack Sennett in the days when that studio had a flock of well known comedians. In 1926 he teamed with George Sidney for the first of the Cohens and Kellys comedies for Universal and the films proved to be big money makers for the studio. Among his films were: *The Cohens and the Kellys in Scotland; Clancy in Wall Street; Around the Corner; The Cohens and the Kellys in Africa; Caught Cheating; The Cohens and the Kellys in Trouble; Dangerous Waters; Circus Girl; The Road to Reno;* and *Breaking the Ice.* Murray retired in 1938 and was a familiar figure at all sporting events and circuses in the area. He died in Los Angeles July 29, 1941 of pneumonia.

Burt Mustin
1884-

Burt Mustin was born Burton Mustin in Pittsburgh, Pennsylvania. He was graduated from Pennsylvania Military Academy in 1903 and spent the next two years in Europe. After a stint as a YMCA secretary during World War I he spent the next twenty-five years in his hometown as an automobile salesman. A gifted singer, he was a part of Pittsburgh's musical scene for many years and also sang on radio. During World War II he retired and moved to Tucson, Arizona. While there, he participated in the local theatre group. In 1951 he was asked to play a small part in "Detective Story" as a janitor and his Hollywood career began at the age of sixty-seven. He has been seen in many television productions including parts on the "Andy Griffith Show"; "Petticoat Junction"; "Mayberry R.F.D."; and "The Funny Side." His films include: *The Lusty Men; Cattle Queen of Montana; Rally Round the Flag Boys; Son of Flubber; Cat Ballou; Cincinnati Kid; Reluctant Astronaut; The Love Bug; The Skin Game;* and *Just across the Street.*

Burt Mustin, right, with Cecil Kellaway in *Just across the Street*.

Carroll O'Connor.

Carroll O'Connor
1924-

After years as an established character actor on stage, screen and television, Carroll O'Connor became a star through his Emmy-winning portrayal of Archie Bunker in the television series, "All in the Family."

Born in New York City of Irish, Roman Catholic background, O'Connor grew up in Forest Hills, Long Island. In 1942 he shipped out as a merchant seaman and served four years. He enrolled at the University of Montana in 1948 majoring in English and developing an interest in drama. On a visit to Ireland in 1950, O'Connor decided to finish school at the National University of Ireland. While in Dublin he acted at the Dublin Gate Theatre. Later he appeared in productions in Cork, Limerick, and Galway.

In 1954 O'Connor returned to New York. Unable to find theatrical work he did substitute teaching. Returning to the University of Montana in 1956, he earned his M.A. degree.

During the late 1950s he finally became established in the theatre playing in such productions as *Ulysses in Nighttown* and *The Big Knife.* Performances on television followed and finally his first film, *Fever in the Blood*, in 1961. During the next eleven years, he appeared in twenty-seven films and became established as one of Hollywood's most versatile character actors.

Film credits include: *Lonely Are the Brave; Cleopatra; Waterhole #3; By Love Possessed; Warning Shot; Marlowe; Death of a Gunfighter; Kelly's Heroes;* and *Doctors' Wives.*

Pat O'Malley
1890-1966

Pat O'Malley was born in Forest City, Pa., in 1890. He began his career in New York on the stage in 1908. He started films there in 1914 (before moving to Hollywood in 1918) where he was under contract to Universal until 1927.

This veteran actor played leading roles in pictures for a number of years and later worked as a character actor in both films and television productions.

O'Malley appeared in over four hundred films, including: *Beloved Enemy; The Fall Guy; Captain Caution; Over My Dead Body; Deep in the Heart of Texas; Night of Nights; Lassie Come Home; Two Yanks in Trinidad; Hollywood Boulevard;* and *Mysterious Crossing.*

Bud Osborne
1884-1964

Bud Osborne became a legend in handling stagecoaches, buckboards, or any type of wagon and when the story called for some wild driving he usually got the job. For many years he also played one of the "bad guys" in countless westerns. He was born Lennie B. Osborne in Oklahoma Territory on July 20, 1884. He learned to ride at an early age. After attending public schools he became a rancher in Chickasha Indian Territory, and later joined the 101 Ranch Wild West Shows, and then the Buffalo Bill Cody's Wild West Shows. Osborne started his film career with the Thomas Ince Company in 1915. In addition to western films he also appeared in many serials, both silent and sound, for such studios as Pathé, Universal, Mascot, Republic and Columbia. His films included; *The Lariat Kid; O'Malley Rides Alone; Bulldog Courage; Song of the Saddle; Guns of the Pecos; Land of Six Guns; Ragtime Cowboy Joe; The Ghost Rider; The Laramie Trail; Border Outlaws;* and *The Hanging Tree.* He died at the Motion Picture Hospital in Woodland Hills, California of a heart attack February 2, 1964.

Pat O'Malley, right, with Judy Canova in *Singin' in the Corn*.

Bud Osborne, left, with Jimmey Wakely and Dub Taylor in *Gun Runner*.

Michael O'Shea

?-1973

Michael O'Shea was born in Connecticut and entered show business at the age of fourteen. His first Broadway play was Maxwell Anderson's *The Eve of St. Mark*, a role he later repeated in the film version. His other film credits included: *Lady of Burlesque; Captain China; Fixed Bayonets; Jack London; Violence; Lady in Manhattan; Man from Frisco; Circumstantial Evidence;* and *Something for the Boys*. In 1947 he married blond actress Virginia Mayo. In the 1950s he frequently appeared on television. On December 4, 1973, he died of an apparent heart attack in Dallas where he was accompanying his wife who was appearing in *40 Carats* at the Dallas Windmill Theatre. O'Shea was scheduled to join the company when it moved to Houston on December 9, 1973.

Michael O'Shea, left, with Julie Bishop in *The Threat*.

Cecil Parker, right, in *I Believe in You*.

Cecil Parker
1897-1971

Cecil Parker, British stage and film actor was born in Hastings, Sussex, and was educated at St. Francis Xavier College, Bruges, Belgium.

He did not make his stage debut until he was twenty-five in *The Merchant of Venice*, (1922), at Eastborne. His London debut came three years later in *The Inheritors*. Parker firmly established himself in the British theatre in 1941 in Noel Coward's *Blithe Spirit*. His New York debut was in 1950 with Edith Evans in *Daphne Laureola*.

Parker made his screen debut in the silent film, *Woman in White* in 1928 and in sound in 1933, *The Silver Spoon*. He also did *The Browning Version* on television. Some of his many film roles are: *Dark Journey; The Lady Vanishes; Caesar and Cleopatra; Quartet; Man in the White Suit; Indiscreet; 23 Paces to Baker Street;* and *The Ladykillers*. One of his rare noncomedy film roles was in Alfred Hitchcock's *Under Capricorn*.

Alice Pearce
1921-1966

Alice Pearce, rubber-faced character actress, was born in New York. She was a latecomer to Broadway, appearing in *New Faces of 1943* three years after graduating from Sarah Lawrence college. She then appeared in such plays as: *On the Town; Look, Ma, I'm Dancing; Bells Are Ringing;* and *Sail Away*, her last Broadway role, before going to Hollywood in 1963.

Miss Pearce also performed in night clubs. Her appearances at the Blue Angel in New York are said to have established a record, an aggregate of sixty-seven weeks.

Her first screen role in Hollywood was in *Kiss Me, Stupid*. Other parts were in such films as: *Disorderly Orderly; Bus Riley's Back in Town; Opposite Sex; Dear Brigette;* and *On the Town*, for which MGM signed her to recreate on film the role of Lucy Schmeeler.

At the time of her death, Miss Pearce was a regular on the "Bewitched" television series, playing a befuddled next door neighbor. Married twice, her first husband was John Rox, composer, and her second, Paul Davis, artist-director.

Alice Pearce, center, with Felicia Farr and John Fiedler in
Kiss Me Stupid.

Joe Penner
1904-1941

Joe Penner became a big name on radio and his expression "Wanna buy a duck?" and "Oh, you nasty man" became household words for his many fans. He became so popular that in 1934 he was voted America's outstanding radio comedian. He was born Josef Pinter in Nagechkereck, Hungary on November 11, 1904. When he was three his father came to America leaving him behind with his grandparents. His father got a job in an automobile plant in Detroit and sent for his youngster three years later. When Penner was twelve years of age he showed promise as a soprano and sang during Liberty Loan Drives and in a boys choir. After high school he went to work at the Ford plant, then sold pianos in a music store. Not satisfied with this work, Penner wanted a stage career, so became an assistant to a mind-reader but was fired and went to Toledo to become a comedian. After changing his name to Penner, he played in burlesque houses and eventually on Broadway. In 1933 he appeared on the Rudy Vallee radio hour and became an instant smash and soon had his own show. Penner went to Hollywood in 1934 and appeared in the following pictures: *College Rhythm*; *Collegiate*; *New Faces of 1937*; *Life of the Party*; *Go Chase Yourself*; *I'm from the City*; *Mr. Doodle Kicks Off*; *The Day the Rookies Wept*; *Millionaire Playboy*; and *The Boys from Syracuse*. He died in his sleep January 10, 1941 while appearing in *Yokel Boy* in Philadelphia. He was only thirty-six years of age.

Joe Penner, center, with Lorraine Krueger and Kay Sutton in *I'm from the City*.

Osgood Perkins
1892-1937

Osgood Perkins was born May 16, 1892 in West Newton, Massachusetts. He appeared in plays at Harvard University, where he was graduated in 1914. In 1915, he enlisted in the army and was a driver with the American Ambulance unit of the French Army. He returned to America in 1916 and worked in a shoe factory. When the United States entered the war he enlisted and became a second lieutenant. In 1924 actor Roland Young got him a job in his first play *Beggars on Horseback*; he had a long stage career thereafter and was very popular with the critics. After making his first appearance in 1926, he was much in demand for films. He was equally at home playing a suave sophisticate or in a sinister, hard-boiled role, such as gangleader "Johnny Lovo" in *Scarface* in 1932. He was the father appearing with Gertrude Lawrence on Broadway September 21, 1937 in *Susan and God*, after the final performance he died of a heart attack. He was the father of actor Anthony Perkins. A few of his films were: *Knockout Reilly*; *Wild, Wild Susan*; *Mother's Boy*; *Tarnished Lady*; *Madame Dubarry*; *Kansas City Princess*; *The President Vanishes*; *Secret of the Chateau*; *I Dream Too Much*; and *Gold Diggers of 1937*.

Osgood Perkins, left, with Paul Muni in *Scarface*.

Nehemiah Persoff, right, with Cliff Stewart and Joseph Cotten in *Walk Softly, Stranger*.

Nehemiah Persoff
1920-

Nehemiah Persoff was born in Jerusalem, Palestine into a family which included two brothers and two sisters. The family came to the United States in 1929. He is the only actor in the family.

Persoff began working with amateur groups in 1939 and in 1940 won a scholarship at the Dramatic Workshop in New York. After appearing there in a number of productions, finally he landed a part in the Broadway production, *Eve of St. Mark*, but he was fired while still in rehearsal. Persoff then entered the army and served from 1942 to 1945.

After the service, Persoff appeared in stock in the East and was then accepted in the Actor's Studio in 1948. Here he was seen by Charles Laughton and hired for a part in *Galileo*. In 1955 he began working in films and has appeared in about twenty-five. His favorite roles have been Albert in *This Angry Age* and Johnny Torio in *Al Capone*. For his one-man show at the Oxford Theatre in Los Angeles in 1971 he received the L.A. Theatre Critics Award. In addition to his work on the stage and in films, he has also appeared on television. His film credits include: *The Hook*; *Fate Is the Hunter*; *Some Like It Hot*; *The Greatest Story Ever Told*; *The Badlanders*; and *Men in War*.

Howard A. Petrie
1907-1968

Character actor and radio-personality, announcer Howard Petrie was born in Beverly, Massachusetts. After a short term as a bank clerk and securities salesman, he visited Boston radio station WBZ to sell securities and left the station with the job as an announcer at the age of twenty-two.

He joined NBC radio in 1930; his first assignment was "Everything Goes" starring Garry Moore. In 1943, Petrie left his position in New York to become the announcer for "The Judy Cannova Show" in Hollywood.

His move to California resulted in the beginning of a new career in motion pictures. He started in films in 1947 and appeared as a featured character in approximately thirty films. He also appeared in numerous television programs including "Bonanza"; "Rawhide"; "Perry Mason"; and "Edge of Night."

His film credits include: *Walk Softly, Stranger; Bend of the River; Carbine Williams; Pony Soldier; Border River; Fort Ti; Rage at Dawn;* and *The Tin Star.*

Howard Petrie, center, with Paul Stewart and Joseph Cotten in *Walk Softly, Stranger.*

John Philliber
1872-1944

John Philliber's best portayal in motion pictures was as "Pop Benson" in United Artists *It Happened Tomorrow* in 1944. In this escapist film he played a newspaper's veteran librarian who after death gives cub reporter Dick Powell copies of the next day's paper for three successive days. It was a poignant role and Philliber made the most of it. Philliber was in show business for nearly fifty years and spent the greater part of his career in touring companies. He finally landed on Broadway in 1942 in *Mr. Sycamore* amd followed this with parts in *The Star Wagon*; *Two on an Island*; and *Winterset*. He died November 6, 1944 in Elkhart, Indiana. His films included: *A Lady Takes a Chance*; *The Imposter*; *Double Indemnity*; *Ladies in Washington*; *Summer Storm*; *Three Is a Family*; *Since You Went Away*; and *Gentle Annie*.

John Philliber, right, with Dick Powell in *It Happened Tomorrow*.

164

Irving Pichel, left, with Otto Kruger in *Dracula's Daughter*.

Irving Pichel
1891-1954

Irving Pichel was born June 24, 1891 in Pittsburgh. He was graduated from Harvard in 1914. He organized community playhouses in several cities and in 1919 joined the Shubert organization as a stage director. He accepted a job from M-G-M to write scripts and after about six months began appearing in films. He became a director and directed such films as: *Happy Land; And Now Tomorrow; A Medal for Benny; Colonel Effingham's Raid; Tomorrow Is Forever; Miracle of the Bells; Mr. Peabody and the Mermaid;* and *Twilight*. He was a member of the theatre arts faculty at University of California at Los Angeles and was a lecturer for several other colleges. In 1953 he was acclaimed for *Martin Luther*. A week before he died (July 13, 1954) of a heart attack, he completed directing a film in Hollywood. Included in his films were: *An American Tragedy; The Miracle Man; Mysterious Rider; Fog Over Frisco; Cleopatra; Three Kids and a Queen; Dracula's Daughter; Armored Car; Jezebel; Juarez;* and *Topper Takes a Trip*.

Francis Pierlot
1875-1955

Francis Pierlot came to Hollywood in 1939 with the idea that he would retire but instead he played many character roles in films. He was born July 15, 1875 in France, came to the United States when he was small, and was raised in Boston. His first connection with show business was when he became a theatre usher at the age of thirteen. Pierlot graduated to the role of an actor and played in vaudeville and had a long career on the Broadway stage. In addition to films he also made many television appearances and was "Mr. Hubert" on the "Jack Carson" television show. He died May 11, 1955 of a heart attack in Hollywood. His many film roles included: *The Captain Is a Lady*; *Submarine Zone*; *Night Monster*; *Mission to Moscow*; *The Very Thought of You*; *A Tree Grows in Brooklyn*; *Two Guys from Milwaukee*; *Philo Vance's Gamble*; *The Dude Goes West*; *The Prisoner of Zenda*; *The Robe*; and *Hit the Hay*.

Francis Pierlot, right, with Forunio Bonanova, Judy Canova, and Ross Hunter in *Hit the Hay*.

Cameron Prud'homme
1892-1967

Cameron Prud'homme, who specialized in father roles was born in Auburn, California. He began his career with the Henry Duffy stock company in San Francisco.

Prud'homme was noted for his performances in the title role of "David Harum," one of the best-known radio soap operas of the 1930s. He also had roles in almost every major radio drama.

His career on the stage was practically a career of playing father to Broadway leading ladies. These included Shirley Booth, Gwen Verdon, and Geraldine Page. Until 1962 he appeared in many television drama shows including: "Robert Montgomery Presents"; "Pulitzer Prize Theatre"; and "Studio One." At one time he appeared in as many as twenty-six shows in an eighteen-week period.

In films since 1930, his many credits included: *The Power and the Prize; Back from Eternity; The Rainmaker; The Cardinal; Doorway to Hell; Soldiers' Plaything; I Like Your Nerve;* and *Honor of the Family.*

Cameron Prud'Homme, right, with Wendell Corey and Lloyd Bridges in *The Rainmaker.*

Dick Purcell
1905-1944

Dick Purcell appeared in a lot of films in just ten short years on the screen. He was born on August 6, 1905 in Greenwich, Connecticut. The handsome Purcell came to films from the stage when he played in *Paths of Glory; Sailor Beware;* and *Men in White.* He signed with Warner Bros. in 1935 and starred or played second leads in seventy films. His starring vehicles were usually "B" type films. Purcell was chosen to play the famous comic strip character, *Captain America* in a serial by Republic released in 1944. He also played District Attorney Grant Gardner and for fifteen chapters he fought with the villainous Lionel Atwill. A few months after the serial was finished he played a round of golf at the Rivera Country Club in Los Angeles on April 10, 1944 and died suddenly of a heart attack. His films included: *Ceiling Zero; Bullets or Ballots; Missing Witnesses; Alcatraz Island; Valley of the Giants; Street of New York; The Bank Dick; Bullets for O'Hara; Torpedo Boat; Aerial Gunner; Timber Queen;* and *Farewell My Lovely.*

Chips Rafferty
1909-1971

Chips Rafferty, whose real name was John Goffage, was born at Broken Hill, a mining town in New South Wales. He took his professional name when his first film role in 1938 called for an Irishman.

His height of six feet six inches earned him slapstick comedy roles in Australia's film industry. Not until given leave from the Royal Australian Air Force to play in wartime morale boosters did he create his most durable role, the lanky, drawling,

Dick Purcell, right, with John Litel and George E. Stone in
Alcatraz Island.

Chips Rafferty in *Double Trouble.*

"Dinkum." He played variations on this theme in most of his roles.

Rafferty worked in both Australian and American post-war films as well as television. Besides film and television roles he had his own film company, Southern International Ltd. He was made a member of the Order of the British Empire by Queen Elizabeth II.

Among his film credits are: *Rats of Tobruk; The Wackiest Ship in the Army; Mutiny on the Bounty; The Overlanders; Kangaroo; The Desert Rats; The Sundowners; Bitter Springs;* and *Kona Coast.*

Ford Rainey
1908-

Born in Mountain Home, Idaho, Rainey began his career in Seattle, Washington in 1932. He

Ford Rainey.

started out in repertory theatre after attending dramatics school. A career in radio followed and then Broadway and off-Broadway productions.

Rainey served in the Coast Guard during World War II and upon discharge stayed on the West Coast. His first motion picture was *White Heat* in 1948 with James Cagney. The most fascinating director he ever worked with was John Ford in *Two Rode Together*. "He (Ford) did more acting off camera than anyone in the picture."

Rainey in addition to films has many television credits to his name. His hobbies are photography and beekeeping. Film credits include: *The Badlanders; The Last Mile; Flaming Star; Parrish; The Sand Pebbles;* and *The Grove.*

Isabel Randolph
1890-1973

Miss Randolph's career spanned the Broadway stage, films, radio, and television. Inactive during the last ten years of her life, Miss Randolph had appeared on the Broadway stage in such productions as *The Noose* and *Bird of Paradise*. She also appeared in a number of Belasco productions.

Following a series of stock and road engagements, she launched her radio career in Chicago as Mrs. Uppington on the "Fibber McGee and Molly" radio series. When the program moved to Hol-

Isabel Randolph, left with Rufe Davis and Shirley Mitchell in *Jamboree*.

lywood in 1939, Miss Randolph went West and remained on the coast.

Her screen roles included both Gene Autry and Roy Rogers films as well as *On Their Own; Yesterday's Heroes;* and *Look Who's Laughing.* Television credits included such shows as "I Love Lucy" and the "Robert Cummings Show."

Herbert Rawlinson
1885-1953

Herbert Rawlinson first saw his name in print on the screen in 1912; he was one of the lucky ones who made the transition from silents to sound. He was born in Brighton, England November 15, 1885. He ran away from home to join the circus and came to the United States in 1910 as manager of the Belasco Stock Company. Rawlinson was on the stage in repertory shows, appeared in vaudeville, and finally on the legitimate stage in New York. He received top billing on Broadway. Rawlinson entered films and became a popular leading man in both features and serials. As he got older he gracefully slipped into character parts as he had a flair for the well-groomed role. Rawlinson appeared in many features and several serials, sometimes as the unlikely villain. He died of cancer July 12, 1953. His films included: *The People's Enemy; Show Them No Mercy; Bullets or Ballots; Mysterious Crossing; Torchy Gets Her Man; Dark Victory; I Wanted Wings; Broadway Big Shot; Colt Comrades; Nabonga; Oklahoma Raiders;* and *Gene Autry and the Mounties.*

George Regas
1890-1940

George Regas was born November 9, 1890 in Sparta, Greece. He first appeared on the Athens stage and came to the United States as Romeo in a Grecian version of *Romeo and Juliet* in New York. Mary Pickford introduced him to films in 1921 in *Love Light* for Universal and he stayed to play characters of many nationalities in more than one hundred films. His credits included: *Blood Money; Viva Villa!; Bulldog Drummond Fights Back; Red Blood of Courage; Rose Marie; The Californians; Mr. Moto Takes a Chance; Code of the Secret Service; The Cat and the Canary;* and *The Adventures of Sherlock Holmes.* He died December 13,1940 in Hollywood after an operation for a throat infection.

Herbert Rawlinson.

Craig Reynolds
1907-1949

Craig Reynolds was born Hugh Enfield on July 15, 1907 in Anaheim, California, and began his career in a drama-art workshop before appearing in vaudeville. He played in a number of little theatre groups including the Pasadena Community

George Regas, center, with Rochelle Hudson and Peter Lorre in *Mr. Moto Takes a Chance.*

Craig Reynolds, left, with Evelyn Ankers in *Queen of Burlesque.*

Playhouse and started his film career under the name of Robert Allen, but when he was signed by a major studio he changed it to Craig Reynolds. He was one of the first Hollywood players to enlist when World War II started. Reynolds was seriously wounded in action and was discharged from the Marine Corps as a lieutenant. Reynolds died October 22, 1949 as a result of injuries received in an automobile accident. He was survived by his actress wife, Barbara Pepper. His busy film career led to roles in: *Stage Struck; Here Comes Carter!; Penrod and Sam; The Great Garrick; Gold Mine in the Sky; The Mystery of Mr. Wong; The Fatal Hour; Nevada; Divorce;* and *Queen of Burlesque.*

Jason Robards Sr.
1892-1963

Jason Robards Sr. was born December 31, 1892 in Hillsdale, Michigan. He attended the New York Dramatic Arts Academy in New York City and first attracted attention when he costarred with Helen Menkin in *Seventh Heaven* in Los Angeles and also appeared on the stage in *Lightnin*. Robards switched to silent films and continued his career through the sound era. On radio he played "Chandu" in "Chandu the Magician." His last public appearance was on Broadway in 1958 in *The Disenchanted*. Robards died April 4, 1963 of a heart attack in Sherman Oaks, California leaving a son to carry on in the theatre and films. Among his many films were: *Abraham Lincoln; Charlie Chan Carries On; The Docks of San Francisco; Sky Patrol; The Master Race; The Falcon's Alibi; Seven Keys to Baldpate; Western Heritage; Rimfire;* and *The Second Woman.*

Jason Robards Sr., left, with Steve Brodie in *Desperate*.

Bill Robinson in *One Mile from Heaven*.

Bill "Bojangles" Robinson
1878-1949

For anyone who ever saw him, who could forget the dancing of Bill Robinson? His personality came across to everyone who ever saw his dancing up and down the stairs with Shirley Temple. He was born Luther Robinson in Richmond, Virginia on May 25, 1878. Robinson began working at the age of eight in a racing stable and rose out of poverty in the South. As a kid, he danced for pennies and became one of the highest paid performers in show business. He toured the vaudeville houses with the act of Cooper and Robinson. In 1921 he got the idea for his stair-dance routine while doing an encore at the Palace in New York. He climbed steadily, rising to a two thousand dollar weekly salary as a musical comedy star. He appeared in many *Blackbirds* revues on Broadway and was a smash hit in the swing version of Gilbert and Sullivan's *The Hot Mikado*. Robinson was always willing to perform for any charity even when he didn't know the organization. He made many donations to the needy and was instrumental in establishing orphanages and scholarships for students. During some years it is estimated he gave four hundred charitable performances. Robinson appeared in many films and staged the dances for the picture *Dimples* in 1936 and taught Shirley Temple several dance routines. His films included: *The Little Colonel; In Old Kentucky; Hooray for Love; One Mile from Heaven; The Littlest Rebel; Rebecca of Sunnybrook Farm; Road Demon; Up the River;* and *Stormy Weather*. Robinson gave up dancing only three months before he died (November 25, 1949).

Hayden Rorke
1910-

A veteran actor of stage, screen, and television, Hayden Rorke appeared in a long list of characterizations. Born in Brooklyn and educated at Brooklyn Prep, Villanova College, and The American Academy of Dramatic Arts, he began his career in

Hayden Rorke.

the theatre as a member of Walter Hampden's Classical Repertory Company touring the United States in 1931. His Broadway debut was in *If Booth Had Missed* in 1932. Since his debut, Rorke has appeared on stage with most major Broadway stars including Katharine Hepburn, Joseph Cotton, Van Heflin, Shirley Booth, Ruth Gordon, Jane Cowl, Constance Colliers, and Gladys Cooper.

As a major personality in movies, Rorke has become familiar to audiences all over the world. He has had featured parts in: *Spencer's Mountain; The Unsinkable Molly Brown; The Night Walker; A House Is Not a Home; The Thrill of It All; Barefoot Executive; I'd Rather Be Rich; Youngbloode Hawk; An American in Paris;* and *Pillow Talk*. Rorke has appeared in over three hundred television shows including three series of which he is best known as Dr. Bellows in "I Dream of Jeannie."

Considered an authority on Bassett hounds, he is well known in the dog-show circuit as a breeder of champions. However, first and foremost, Hayden Rorke is an actor.

Anthony Ross
1906-1955

Anthony Ross was a native New Yorker, was graduated from Brown University, and studied at the Sorbonne in Paris. He made his Broadway debut in 1932 in *Whistling in the Dark*. Other stage triumphs were *The Twelfth Night*,1940; and *Arsenic and Old Lace*, 1941; *Winged Victory*, 1943; and *The Glass Menagerie*. Ross was an impressive actor who was very well thought of by the critics and entered films in 1950. His outstanding role was as "Phil Cook," the heartless producer in *The Country Girl* in 1954. The same year he played Lt. Detective Richard Hale on television in the mystery series, "The Telltale Clue." Among his other films were: *The Perfect Strangers; The Gunfighter; The Vicious Years; The Skipper Surprised His Wife; Between Midnight and Dawn; The Flying Missile; On Dangerous Ground; Taxi; Girls in the Night;* and *Rogue Cop*. In 1955 he was playing the tipsy professor in *Bus Stop* on Broadway. On October 26,1955, a few hours after playing this featured role at the Music Box Theatre he suffered a fatal heart attack.

Anthony Ross, center, with Robert Walker in *The Skipper Surprised His Wife*.

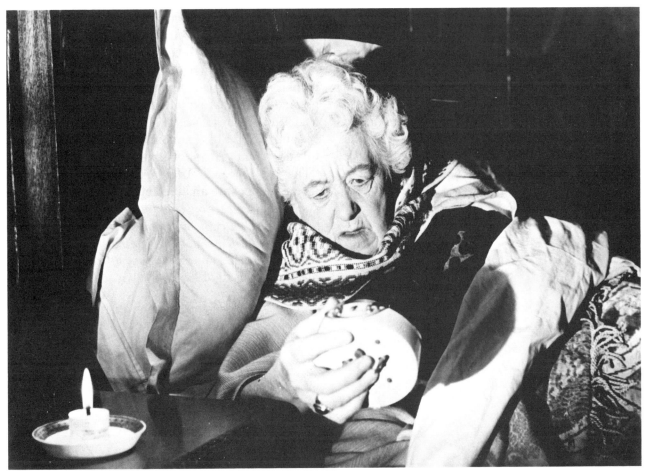

Margaret Rutherford in *Murder at the Gallop*.

Dame Margaret Rutherford
1892-1972

Dame Margaret Rutherford was the creator of a notable gallery of film and stage eccentrics. Born in London, the only child of William and Florence Rutherford, she made her debut at the age of eight, though it took her a quarter century before she got on the adult stage.

Dame Margaret spent six years studying the piano which she later taught after receiving licentiate of the Royal College of Music. She also studied elocution and won a degree in the subject which she taught along with piano.

When she was thirty-three, she came into a small inheritance, she gave up teaching and joined the Old Vic as a student. Temporarily, she had to return to teaching, but finally in 1929, she caught on in repertory in the provinces, ending up in London in 1933. One of her first hits was as Madame Arcati, the bicycling medium in Noel Coward's *Blithe Spirit*, which she played on the London stage and in the film.

She first visited the United States in 1947 with John Gielgud, playing Lady Bracknell in *The Importance of Being Earnest*. Dame Margaret's film career made her known throughout the world as she appeared in a succession of great postwar British film comedies as: *Blithe Spirit; Passport to Pimlico; Miranda; The Mouse on the Moon; The Happiest Days of Your Life;* and *The Importance of Being Earnest*. She became the obvious choice as Jane Marple in Agatha Christie thrillers; and the Duchess of Brighton in *The V. I. P.'s* for which she won her Oscar as Best Supporting Actress.

For her services to the theatre she was named an officer of the Order of the British Empire in 1961. And in 1967, Queen Elizabeth made her a Dame of the Empire. The whimsical, the fey, the dotty, the bombastic—these were the images she projected to the delight of millions. "Everbody says one thing or the other—either I'm just what they expected or just the opposite," she remarked. "But I'm not displeased when people think I'm like my eccentric ladies—I love playing them." The favorite character actress on both sides of the Atlantic died at her home in Chalfont, St. Peter, Buckinghamshire, survived by her husband, the actor and producer, Stringer Davis, and four adopted children.

Basil Ruysdael
1888-1960

Basil Ruysdael was born July 24, 1888 in New Jersey. In his early career he was a leading basso at the Met where he appeared with Enrico Caruso and Geraldine Farrar. He also coached future opera stars such as Lawrence Tibbett. Ruysdael then turned to the Broadway stage in 1918. In 1929 he began his film career with the Marx Bros., in their first film, *The Cocoanuts*. He then left films and became a top radio announcer in the thirties and forties. Among his shows were "Jack Benny" and "The Hit Parade." In 1949 he returned to films where he became an able actor with a fine voice in such films as: *File on Thelma Jordan*; *Pinky*; *Come to the Stable*; *Broken Arrow*; *Raton Pass*; *Boots Malone*; *The Blackboard Jungle*; *Jubal*; *The Last Hurrah*; and his last, *The Story of Ruth*. Ruysdael died October 10, 1960 in Hollywood.

Basil Ruysdael, left, with William Holden and Stanley Clements in *Boots Malone*.

Irene Ryan, right, with Robert Kent in *Hot Rhythm*.

Irene Ryan
1906-1973

Miss Ryan was an actress from the age of ten, when she began her colorful career winning three dollars on amateur night at San Francisco's Valencia Theatre, singing "Pretty Baby." For years she performed in vaudeville as a team with her first husband, Tim Ryan as "Tim and Irene." They also had a radio show for many years. She then had feature roles on the old Bob Hope and Rudy Vallee radio shows.

In 1962 Miss Ryan got the role of "Granny" in "The Beverly Hillbillies." The show ran for nine seasons and became one of the most successful television series ever. Miss Ryan did not make her Broadway debut until the last nine months of her career when she appeared in the hit musical, *Pippin*. For her portrayal of a regal but lusty medieval grandmother in *Pippin*, she won a Tony award.

Miss Ryan, who in recent years had become a millionaire through savings and investments, founded the Irene Ryan Foundation to establish annual scholarships to encourage young people in their acting endeavors.

Though best known as "Granny Clampett," she spent a lifetime in character parts in radio and films. Among her many film credits are: *San Diego I Love You; Blackbeard the Pirate; Melody for Three; Spring Reunion; Meet Me after the Show;* and *Hot Rhythm*. She died April 26, 1973 of a stroke.

Howard St. John
1905-1974

Howard St. John did extensive work as a character actor on Broadway, in films and on television, usually as an executive, father, or political big-wig.

St. John appeared on the stage since 1925 in more than a score of plays, among them: *Jane; Teahouse of the August Moon; The Fatal Weakness; The Late George Apley*. He appeared in Garson Kanin's *Born Yesterday* both on Broadway and with Judy Holliday in the film version. St. John also played the part of General Bullmoose in *L'il Abner* for two seasons at the St. James Theatre and again repeated the role on the screen. He was a leading man for such stars as Ina Claire, Ruth Gordon, and Edna Best.

St. John appeared in numerous films adapting his personality equally well to comedy or drama. His roles include: *One, Two, Three; Lover Come Back; Sanctuary; Cry for Happy; Madison Avenue; LaFayette (George Washington); Straitjacket; David Harding; Counterspy;* and *The Tender Trap*.

Howard St. John.

Natalie Schafer

Born in New York, Miss Schafer grew up with her mother and stepfather. She was enrolled in school at the Hamilton Institute in New York. Not being allowed to study drama, she studied costume designing. Under the influence of Katherine Cornell, who taught at the school, Miss Schafer changed her plans and became a drama student.

Given an early opportunity for a job with the Theatre Guild, she had to refuse because of her parents and for a time had to do other work. Not able to resist the stage, she quit her job and signed for ten weeks of stock in Atlanta. This led to Broadway and a number of plays. In 1934 she married Louis Calhern and together they worked in a number of productions. *AGE, 73 (1980)*

While on Broadway she was signed by MGM and made her film debut in *Marriage Is a Private Affair*. She refused a long-term contract and divided her time between the stage and films. In 1959 she made her first appearance on television and many guest spots followed. These finally culminated in the television series, *Gilligan's Island*. Her career has continued with parts in plays, films and television. Among her many film credits are: *Keep Your Powder Dry; The Time of Your Life; The Snake Pit; Take Care of My Little Girl; Anastasia; The Girl Next Door; Bernadine; Back Street;* and *Susan Slade*.

William Schallert
1922-

William Schallert was born in Los Angeles. His father was a drama editor for the *L.A. Times* and his mother, a publicist, wrote for fan magazines and movie reviews.

William Schallert's career began with The Circle Theatre in Hollywood. His first movie was a bit role in *The Foxes of Harrow*, 1947. Other films to follow were: *Red Badge of Courage; Man from Planet X; The High and the Mighty; Some Came Running;* and *Smoke Signal*.

Natalie Schafer, left, with Brian Aherne in *Susan Slade*.

William Schallert.

Schallert was also doing most of the usual television material in these years and continued to work on the stage. A big step in his career occurred in 1959 when he was signed to work for the "Dobie Gillis" television program. By 1966 he was a well-established and recognized actor in Hollywood. His favorite picture to date is *Lonely Are the Brave*. Mr. Schallert won an Obie award for his off-Broadway performance in *Trial of the Catonville Nine*, later playing in the film version.

According to Schallert: "I've had the most fun and success in television and on the stage." Married to actress Lia Wagger, they have four sons, none of which has shown any serious inclinations toward acting. His chief hobby is music — playing the piano, singing and composing. Other important films credits include: *Charley Varrick*; *Heat of the Night*; *Hour of the Gun*; and *Collosus: The Forbin Project*.

Victor Sen Yung.

Victor Sen Yung
1915-

Victor Sen Yung, born in San Francisco of parents from Canton, China, worked his way through school as a "houseboy," starting at the age of twelve. He was graduated from the University of California with an A.B. in economics.

With no early acting experience, he was cast in the role of Charlie Chan's No. 2 son in the *Charlie Chan* series, as the direct result of a screen test given to him when he approached 20th Century-Fox in the capacity of a salesman.

With only a degree in economics Sen Yung enrolled in an actors studio and to round out his knowledge of motion pictures took courses at the California Graduate School of Cinema Arts.

His favorite roles have included Ong Chi Seng in *The Letter*; Jimmy Chan in the *Chan* Series; Hop Sing in television's "Bonanza"; and Sammy Fong in the stage and film productions of *Flower Drum Song*.

To survive and continue work in the entertainment field of necessity he has done a variety of jobs including restaurant management, selling men's wear, frozen food production, and product promotion for processed Chinese food products. He is also the author of the *Great Wok Cookbook*.

Other film credits include: *Across the Pacific*; *The Left Hand of God*; and *A Flea in the Ear*. He was also in: *Lost Horizon, The General Died at Dawn*; and *The Good Earth*.

Gustav Von Seyffertitz
1863-1943

George Sidney
1887-1945

Gustav von Seyffertitz was born August 4, 1863 in Tyrol, Austria. He began his acting career on the stage prior to a thirty year film career. In addition to his acting chores he was also associated with D. W. Griffith and directed for Paramount. During World War I when a German name was not popular he changed his name to Butler Clonebaugh. When the war was over he resumed his rightful name and continued to play character parts until four years prior to his death on December 25, 1943. His films included: *The Canary Murder Case; Dishonored; Shanghai Express; Rasputin and the Empress; Queen Christina; Mystery Liner; Little Men; She; In Old Chicago;* and *Nurse Edith Cavell.*

George Sidney was born on March 15, 1877 in Hungary and came to the United States when he was five. By the age of twelve he was already appearing in music halls and in vaudeville skits. He was teamed with Lou Heyman and then with Harry Von Tilzer who became a famous song writer. Sidney developed the character "Busy Izzy" and played in four of these productions. After coming to Hollywood in 1925 his film work included the Potash and Perloutter series. Sidney teamed with Charlie Murray in 1926 to make the popular "Cohens and Kellys" for Universal. They teamed in this series for several years. His other film work included: *The Cohens and the Kellys in Scotland; Caught Cheating; Around the Corner, High Pressure; The Cohens and the Kellys in Hollywood; Rafter Romance; Manhattan Melodrama; Diamond Jim;* and *Good Old Soak.* He died April 29, 1945.

Gustav von Seyffertitz, center, with Richard Alexander, left, in *The Mysterious Lady.*

George Sidney in *Cohens and Kellys in Hollywood*.

Art Smith, right, with Robert Montgomery in *Ride the Pink Horse*.

Art Smith
1899-1973

Art Smith was a prominent Broadway actor who made his acting debut in Chicago in 1924. He first appeared on Broadway in 1930 with Bette Davis in *Broken Dishes*. Smith won the New York Critics award for his performance in *Rocket to the Moon* and won favorable notices for his other stage roles.

He made his film debut in 1943 in *Edge of Darkness* with Errol Flynn and among his many films were : *The Black Parachute*; *A Tree Grows in Brooklyn*; *Moon over Montana*; *Brute Force*; *Arch of Triumph*; *A Double Life*; *Manhandled*; *Quicksand*; *In a Lonely Place*; and *Half Angel*. His last appearance was on television in "Do Not Go Gentle Into That Good Night" in 1967. Smith died of a heart attack February 24, 1973 in West Babylon, Long Island.

Kent Smith
1907-

Kent Smith was born in New York City, was graduated from Philip Exeter Academy, and attended Harvard University. He first appeared on the stage assisting the Great Blackstone. There followed various stage productions and stocks. On Broadway, parts included *Heat Lightning; Dodsworth; Caesar and Cleopatra; Antony and Cleopatra;* and many others.

Smith made his film debut in *Cat People* for RKO in 1942. Other films have included *Hitler's Children; The Spiral Staircase; Nora Prentiss; My Foolish Heart; Voice of the Turtle; Sayonara;* and *Paula.* His television credits include the series "Profiles in Courage"; "Death Takes a Holiday"; and Hallmark Hall of Fame's "Richard II."

Distinguished actor of stage, screen and television, Smith's favorite roles are that of the doctor in *Nora Prentiss* and Charles Evans Hughes in the television series *Profiles in Courage.* His hobbies are croquet and music.

Kent Smith, left, with Patricia Owens and Martha Scott in *Sayonara*.

Olan Soulé.

Olan Soulé
1909-

Olan Soulé was born in La Harpe, Illinois, and educated there and in the public schools of Des Moines, Iowa. The first seven years of his career were spent in tent shows and resident stocks. In 1933 Mr. Soulé started in radio in Chicago on WGN where he was featured on such shows as: "Little Orphan Annie"; "Jack Armstrong"; "Bachelor's Children"; and the "First Night Program."

In 1947, Soulé moved to Hollywood where shortly he received his first part in a motion picture—an off-camera radio announcer, whose voice was heard over a speaker. Since his film debut he has appeared in over 150 pictures with television appearances on practically every major program (some 190) featured on television starting in 1948.

Very active in professional organizations and the Masonic Lodge, it is interesting to note, that when Soulé was born his parents, who were Worthy Matron and Patron of the Eastern Star, picked his two names, Olan and Evart, so his initials would be OES for Order of Eastern Star.

Among Olan Soulé's film credits are: *Destination Big House*; *Cuban Fireball*; *Call Me Madam*, and *Dragnet*.

Arthur Space
1908-

Arthur Space was born in New Brunswick, New Jersey. The family was "low middle class," victorian and religious. Although always uncomfortable in school, he graduated from high school where he was discovered by a professor from the New

Arthur Space, left, with June Vincent in *The Lone Wolf and His Lady*.

Jersey College for Women. While in high school he was put into a number of their plays.

Following graduation, Space involved himself in a number of activities. He went to sea, worked for the Pennsylvania Railroad, W.P.A., seafood restaurants, fishmarkets, and as a clam opener. During these years acting was never far from his life. Space played leads in productions throughout New Jersey, summer stocks, and on the subway circuit in and around New York. Staying in New York, he made Broadway in *Night of January 16th*. Subsequently, he appeared in such plays as *Three Men on a Horse* and *Accent on Youth*.

Out of acting work during the depression, Space decided to go to Hollywood, where after a short time, he got his break and with that initial start has appeared in over 150 pictures and two hundred television productions. In these he has appeared with most of the major stars and child actors. Among Space's many films are: *Random Harvest*; *Wilson*; *Spirit of St. Louis*; *Tortilla Flat*; *Our Vines Have Tender Grapes*; *Son of Lassie*; *20 Million Miles to Earth*; *The Big Noise*; and *Fuller Brush Man*.

Hope Summers.

Hope Summers
1902-

Hope Summers was born in Mattoon, Illinois, into a family which included a prominent physician, a member of Congress (father), and two brothers who had successful business careers and later entered the Diplomatic Corps.

After leaving college, she had one year with the Peoria, Illinois Community Theatre. Her first professional acting job was with the Harry Duffy Stock Company in Seattle, Washington. In 1927 Miss Summers returned to her alma mater, Northwestern University, to teach.

In 1939 she entered the field of radio in Chicago, playing nearly every show originating there. While in Chicago, Miss Summers founded two stock companies in which she both produced and acted.

Arriving in Hollywood in 1956, she began to appear quite successfully in a number of films. Included in her film credits are: *Black Patch*; *I Want to Live*; *Parrish*; *The Couch*; *Inherit the Wind*; *Children's Hour*; *Hallelujah Trail*; and *The Ghost and Mr. Chicken*.

Throughout her career the personal relationships, the fun, the stimulation are what she remembers the most. To her fans she has been a truly fine versatile actress.

Carl (Alfalfa) Switzer
1926-1959

The skinny kid with the jumping Adam's apple, freckle face, wide eyes and soup-bowl haircut, Carl Switzer was a favorite with movie goers as a star in the *Our Gang* and *Reg'lar Fellers* comedies.

Switzer began his movie career in 1933. He and his young colleagues pranced through a long series of *Our Gang* comedies and then, as they grew older,

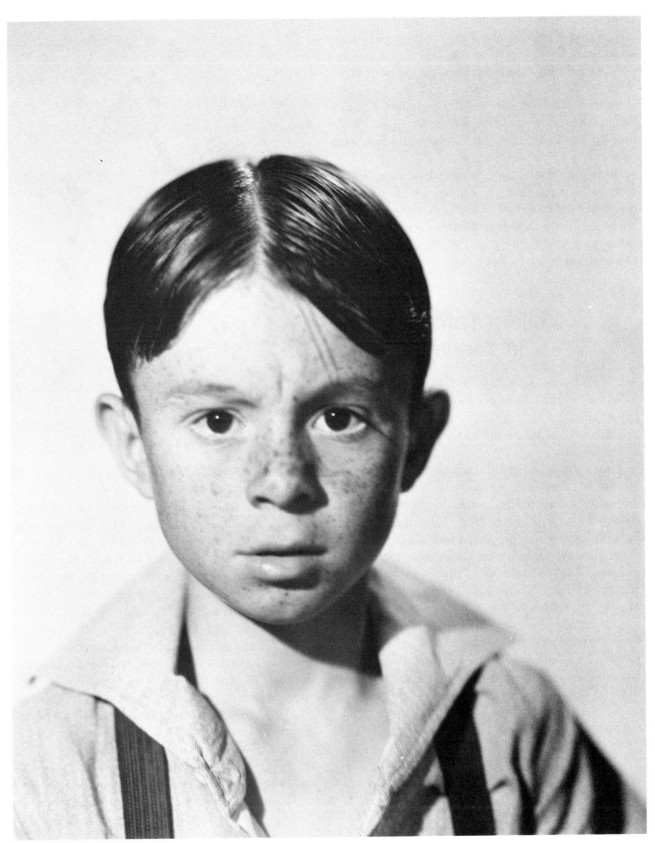

Carl "Alfalfa" Switzer.

appeared in the *Reg'lar Fellers* series. In addition some of Switzer's films in the early period were: *Mrs. Wiggs of the Cabbage Patch*; *Henry and Dizzy*; and *The War against Mrs. Hadley*.

After 1942 his career eclipsed, along with many other child stars. He continued to act, but parts were few. His later film credits included: *The Defiant Ones*; *Letter to Three Wives*; *Going My Way*; *Track of the Cat*; *State of the Union*; and *Big Town Scandal*.

During his last years Switzer had some minor scrapes with the law. A year before his death he was wounded in a mysterious sniper shooting near his home. He was shot to death in San Francisco, January, 1959, as the result of an argument with another man over money.

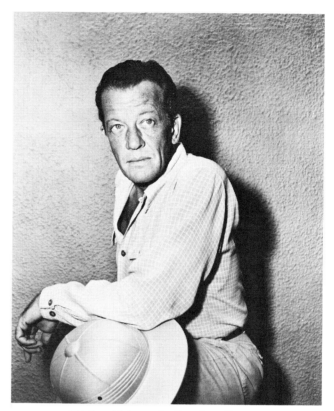

William Talman in *Uranium Boom*.

William Talman
1917-1968

William Talman was born in Detroit. As a youth, he founded an acting club while attending Cranbrook school in Michigan. Later he studied theatre at Dartmouth.

After college he played stock and worked at various jobs (sales clerk, tennis pro, master of ceremonies). Going to New York, he first played on Broadway in *Of Mice and Men*. Talman found work in Hollywood where he played heavies in a number of movies. As an actor he became best known to millions of television fans as the district attorney, Hamilton Burger, who lost every case to Perry Mason. (CANCER)

Talman's appearances in films included roles in : *One Minute to Zero*; *The Hitchhiker*; *Smoke Sign*; *Woman on Pier 13*; *I Married a Communist*; *Red, Hot, and Blue*; *The Kid from Texas*; and his last film, *The Ballad of Josie*, with Doris Day. He won an Academy Award nomination for his role in *The Hitchhiker*.

Ernest Torrence
1878-1933

Ernest Torrence was a tall, rugged, rawboned individual who looked every bit as villainous as the roles he played. He is best remembered for his portrayal of the homicidal maniac in the classic *Tol'able David* in 1921. As good as he was on the screen he was an equally fine musician. Torrence was born in Edinburgh, Scotland June 26, 1878. As a young man he studied music at the Edinburgh Academy of Music, The Conservatorum in Stuttgart, Germany, and the Royal Academy of Music in London. In 1900 he won the Royal Academy's medal for operatic singing and the next year he was operatic baritone of the Savoy Opera Company. During the next ten years he appeared in many musical comedies. Henry King, the director, saw him on Broadway and signed him for *Tol'able David* and he stayed on the screen thereafter. Torrence was the sinister "Dr. Moriarity" in *Sherlock Holmes*; "Captain Hook" in *Peter Pan*; and Ivan in *The Cossacks*. Even though he was the most ferocious villain of the silent screen he could also play the sympathetic roles as he did as the scout in *The Covered Wagon*. He continued his career into sound films and had just completed a part in *I Cover the Waterfront* and was going to visit

Ernest Torrence.

Joseph Turkel in *Paths of Glory*.

his native Scotland when he became ill. Torrence died May 15, 1933 after a gall bladder operation. His brother David Torrence was also a fine actor. His sound films included: *Officer O'Brien; Call of the Flesh; Shipmates; Fighting Caravans; Sporting Blood; Cuban Love Song; Sherlock Holmes; Hypnotized;* and *The Masquerader.*

Lee Van Cleef.

Joseph Turkel
1927-

Joseph Turkel was born in Brooklyn, New York, and spent his formative years of schooling there. At the age of ten he played the Prince on radio in *Let's Pretend.*

At the age of sixteen Joe quit school and joined the Merchant Marines, traveling all over the world. After leaving the Merchant Marines he joined the United States Army for eighteen months. Upon discharge from the army, Turkel attended Carnegie Hall Theatre in New York for two and one-half years. He then started doing off-Broadway plays from which he was brought to Hollywood to do *City across the River* for Universal-International. Returning to New York, Turkel began doing television and worked all the major shows. After a year he returned to Hollywood to work in television and feature films. His many film roles included: *Purple Gang; Man Crazy; The Killing; Paths of Glory; Friendly Persuasion; Boy and the Pirates; The Vikings; The Glass Wall; Portrait of a Mobster; Warlock;* and *The Sand Pebbles.*

Joe Turkel is not the only one of his family to be associated with the arts; his mother sang at the Metropolitan Opera and his father was a painter. He has many hobbies, enjoys sports and likes classical and jazz music.

Lee Van Cleef
1925-

Lee Van Cleef was born in Somerville, New Jersey, on January 9, 1925. After graduation from high school in 1942 he joined the United States Navy where he served on subchasers and minesweepers. After his discharge from the navy he served as an assistant manager in a summer camp and had a brief career as an accountant before joining a little theatre group. His first screen role was as one of the killers, Jack Colby, in the classic western, *High Noon.* Van Cleef's menacing features won him countless roles as the villain in many westerns both on television and in the movies. In 1967 he received second billing in *For a Few Dollars More* and this led to leading roles in several Italian-Spanish films. His star billing left a void among the badmen of the screen. Other films include: *Vice Squad; Gypsy Colt; Ten Wanted Men; Treasure of Ruby Hills; Gunfight at the O.K. Corral; The Man Who Shot Liberty Valance; Death Rides a Horse;* and *Sabata.*

Harold Vermilyea
1889-1958

Harold Vermilyea had a diversified career. He was a secretary to United States Senator Robert L. Owen and secretary to playwright Augustus Thomas. His first Broadway role was in *The Lion and the Horse* in 1914. He appeared in many other Broadway productions and in World War I he served as a captain in the United States Army. In the 1930s he spent a great deal of time on radio, appearing with Maude Adams in a series and playing a leading part on the Rudy Vallee show. From 1940 to 1945 he was director of the American Theatre Wings Victory Players. After the war was over he appeared in many films and was a frequent visitor on prime television shows. Vermilyea was born in New York City on October 10, 1889 and died January 8, 1958. Films in which he appeared included: *O.S.S.*; *Gentlemen's Agreement*; *The Big Clock*; *The Emperor Waltz*; *The Miracle of the Bells*; *Sorry, Wrong Number*; *Manhandled*; *Chicago Deadline*; *Edge of Doom*; and *Finders Keepers*.

Harold Vermilyea, left, with Julia Adams in *Finders Keepers*.

Charles Wagenheim
1901-

Born in Newark, New Jersey of immigrant parents, Charles Wagenheim became an actor because of shyness. After being injured in World War I, the government gave Wagenheim an opportunity to study for a profession. He selected dramatics, attending the American Academy of Dramatic Arts in New York.

After graduation in 1923 with classmates Spencer Tracy, Kay Johnson and Pat O'Brien, he toured the United States with a Shakespearean troup. Wagenheim then returned to New York and Broadway appearing in a number of productions, nine of them George Abbott's.

In 1938 he went to Hollywood. His first film was with Liz Scott in *The Company She Keeps*. In 1939 Hitchcock selected Wagenheim for a part in *Foreign Correspondent*. Both small parts and featured parts followed in over three hundred films and one hundred television shows. Typed for winos, bums, hoboes, and "bedbug" characters, he has kept busy over the years. Wagenheim's favorite roles were the assassin in *Foreign Correspondent* and Paul in *Beneath the Twelve Mile Reef*. Additional film credits include: *Sin Town; Colonel Effingham's Raid; The House on 92nd Street; Canyon Crossroads; Cry of the City; Summer Storm; Dark Corner;* and *Scudda' Hoo! Scudda Hay!*

Charles Wagenheim in *Foreign Correspondent*.

197

Ray Walston in *Paint Your Wagon*.

Ray Walston
1914-

Bryant Washburn
1889-1963

Walston was born in Laurel, Mississippi. A character comedian, he began his stage experience with Margo Jones Community Players in Houston, Texas, from 1938 to 1942. From 1945 to 1955 he appeared on Broadway in various productions as: *Front Page*; *Summer and Smoke*; *South Pacific*; and *Damn Yankees*.

Walston made his film debut in 1957 in *Kiss Them for Me* with Cary Grant and Jayne Mansfield. Films to follow were: *Say One for Me*; *Tall Story*; *The Apartment*; *Wives and Lovers*; *Kiss Me, Stupid*; *Caprice*; and *Paint Your Wagon*. Favorite roles include Luther Billis in *South Pacific* and the Devil in *Damn Yankees*. Recently he has been seen in the television series, "My Favorite Martian."

An excellent cook, Walston is married and has one daughter, Kate.

Bryant Washburn was born in Chicago, Illinois April 28, 1889. In 1914 he entered films after a brief career on the eastern stage. He made the famous Skinner comedies for Essanay studios and in 1918 he was signed by Paramount. In 1921 he was voted one of the top-fifteen male stars at the box office. With the advent of sound he turned to character roles that needed the appearance of a distinguished gentleman. In 1941 he played one of five scientist suspects in one of Republic's best serials, *The Adventures of Captain Marvel* starring Tom Tyler. Among his other film credits were: *Mystery Train*; *Exposure*; *The Devil's Mate*; *The Return of Chandu*; *Danger Ahead*; *Conflict*; *Million Dollar Racket*; *Stagecoach*; *Sin Town*; *Carson City Cyclone*; and *West of the Pecos*. He became an advance man for Mike Todd after his retirement in films. He died in Hollywood of a heart ailment on April 30, 1963.

Bryant Washburn, right, with Bud Osborne, Jack O'Shea, Morgan Flowers, and Stuart Hamblen in *Carson City Cyclone*.

Robert Watson
1888-1965

Leon (Abner) Weaver
1882-1950

Robert Watson Knucher was a native of Springfield, Illinois and became a vaudeville comedian. He also appeared in shows as "The Demi-Virgin" and "Cross My Heart." Although he had many film roles Watson gained his greatest fame portraying Adolph Hitler in such films as: *The Devil with Hitler; Hitler; Dead or Alive; The Hitler Gang;* and *Nazty Nuisance.* He died May 22, 1965. Other films included: *The Miracle of Morgan's Creek; It Ain't Hay; Practically Yours; Duffy's Tavern; Hold That Blonde;* and *Night and Day.*

Leon Weaver was born in Ozark, Missouri, August 12, 1882. He was the first tent-show rural exhibitor in Missouri. He was the older, homespun member of a comedy team that toured vaudeville for many years. Weaver teamed with his brother Frank, better known as "Cicero" and Frank's wife June, better known as "Elviry" and they formed an act known as "The Arkansas Travelers," then simply "The Weaver Bros. and Elviry." They started together in 1914 and became the most successful of all the hillbilly acts in vaudeville playing

Robert Watson, left, with Victor Varconi in *The Hitler Gang*.

**Leon Weaver, top, with Frank Weaver and Louise Fazenda
in *Swing Your Lady*.**

James Westerfield in *Away All Boats*.

the Palace in New York and two trips to Europe. Although Leon played the violin, banjo, and guitar he was better known for introducing the first "musical saw" to vaudeville. Although the team preferred traveling the circuit they made eleven films from 1938 to 1942. Leon died of a heart attack May 27, 1950 one day after being divorced by his wife. His films included: *Swing Your Lady; Down in Arkansas; Jeepers Creepers; In Old Missouri; Grande Ole Opry; Friendly Neighbors; Arkansas Judge; Mountain Moonlight; Tuxedo Junction; Shepherd of the Ozarks;* and *Mountain Rhythm.*

James Westerfield
1913-1971

James Westerfield was a burly character who specialized in tough-cop roles. Active on Broadway, in films and on television, Westerfield also directed and produced.

He won the New York Drama Critics Award in 1948 and 1949 as a best supporting actor in the Broadway plays *The Madwoman of Chaillot* and *Detective Story.*

As a director he produced more than fifty musicals in his own summer musical tent in Danbury, Connecticut. He also appeared with the Detroit Civic Light Opera and the San Francisco and Los Angeles Light Opera Companies. Westerfield's first break was in Max Reinhardt's production of *Faust* in the Hollywood Bowl. He also had numerous television drama credits on "Television Playhouse" and "Playhouse 90."

His films included: *On the Waterfront; True Grit; Blue; A Man Called Gannon; That Funny Feeling;* and his last role in the Mexican-made *Arde (Burn).*

Nydia Westman
1902-1970

Born into a theatrical family, the daughter of actor-composer Theodore Westman and actress-

Nydia Westman in *Ladies Should Listen*.

playwright Lily Wren Westman, Nydia Westman had a successful career in the theatre, films, and television.

She first appeared in her family's act, *Troubles of Joy*, and debuted, at sixteen, on Broadway in John Golden's *Pigs*. Other roles on Broadway included: *Seventh Heaven; Lysistrata; Madwoman of Chaillot;* and *Life with Father*. Miss Westman was also a summer stock regular. She won an Obie in 1958 for Samuel Becket's *Endgame*.

Her film debut was in the 1932 feature *Manhattan Towers*. Many other screen credits followed including: *Pennies from Heaven; Velvet Touch; Craig's Wife; The Cat and the Canary; Late George Apley;* and *For Love or Money*. Her television credits included such series as "Perry Mason" and "Alfred Hitchcock."

Bert Wheeler
1895-1968

Born Albert Jerome Wheeler in Patterson, New Jersey, this comedian of stage, screen, and television for fifty-seven years made generations of Americans laugh.

Wheeler was a teen-age vaudeville hoofer playing in Omaha when he broke the ankle that started him on the road to a comedy career. Ultimately he became a fifteen hundred dollars a week headliner in vaudeville and for seven years was a leading comic in the Ziegfeld Follies. When the Ziegfeld revue, *Rio Rita*, was made into a movie, Wheeler embarked on another career.

Bert Wheeler, left, with Robert Woolsey in *Girl Crazy*.

With Robert Woolsey he formed a movie comedy team that starred in thirty pictures. Among the titles of pictures they worked in were: *Half Shot at Sunrise; Cracked Nuts; Hook, Line, and Sinker; Caught Plastered; Peach O'Reno; Hold 'Em Jail;* and *Girl Crazy.* Their last film was *On Again-Off Again* in 1937. As a single act following Woolsey's death, Wheeler never again made a picture. He returned to vaudeville revues and did radio and television. His love for the theatre continued throughout his life. In 1966 a new theatre named for him opened on Broadway.

Wheeler was married and divorced four times. His only child, Patricia, born of his marriage to Bernice Speer, died only two weeks before her father.

Sir Donald Wolfit
?-1968

Outstanding as a classical actor, Sir Donald Wolfit worked in such varied fields as musical comedy and motion pictures. Born Donald Woolfitt in Norringhamshire, he became a student teacher in a boarding school to pay for elocution lessons. He joined various touring companies playing more than fifty parts.

His London debut was in 1924 as a Negro servant in *The Wandering Jew.* He first drew critical attention in Ashley Dukes' *Such Men Are Dangerous,* in 1928 and with the Old Vic in 1929. During the Battle for Britain he became famous for "lunchtime" performances of Shakespeare during the height of the blitz.

Knighted in 1957 for service to the theatre, his list of films include: *Becket; Drake of England; Lawrence of Arabia; Pickwick Papers; I Accuse; The Angry Hills; Svengali;* and *Room at the Top.*

Married three times, his first two unions ended in divorce. He married Rosalind Iden-Payne in 1948 and she, as Rosalind Iden, played opposite him in many productions.

Donald Wolfit in *Decline and Fall . . . of a Bird Watcher*.

Louis Wolheim.

Louis Wolheim
1881-1931

Louis Wolheim seemed to leave two lasting impressions to the movie fan. First, his unsightly features would classify him as one of the ugliest of all screen actors. Second, anyone who ever saw him in *All Quiet on the Western Front* will not forget his role as Katczinsky, the compassionate soldier of the trenches of World War I. Wolheim was born March 28, 1881 in New York City of Jewish parents. He was graduated from Cornell University with a degree in Mechanical Engineering. He appeared in several plays. Wolheim's most popular role was the lead in *The Hairy Ape* in 1922 and as Captain Flagg in *What Price Glory?* in 1924. He also tried his hand at writing and also directed *Sin Ship* in 1931. His films included: *Dr. Jekyll and Mr. Hyde; Orphans of the Storm; Sherlock Holmes; Wolf Song; Frozen Justice; Condemned; The Ship from Shanghai; Danger Light; The Silver Horde;* and *Gentleman's Fate.* Wolheim died of cancer on February 18, 1931.

Monty Woolley
1888-1963

Monty Woolley will best be remembered in *The Man Who Came to Dinner* and for his splendid white Van Dyke and flaring moustache. He was born Edgar Montillion Woolley on August 17, 1888 in New York. His father owned the fashionable Grand Union Hotel in Saratoga Springs. After high school he entered Yale in 1907 and while there formed a lifelong friendship with Cole Porter. After receiving his masters degree he furthered his education at Harvard and returned to Yale as an English instructor. During World War I he served in France as a lieutenant and upon his return he joined the Yale faculty as an assistant professor of drama. Woolley later became a successful director on Broadway and was a natural wit who became a well known man about town and who was always invited to the best parties. He achieved theatrical fame in *The Man Who Came to Dinner* on Broadway; in 1941 he appeared in the successful film version again as the world famous lecturer, Sheridan Whiteside, who was immobilized by a leg fracture in a small town in Ohio. His first film was in 1937 in *Live, Love, and Learn* and he gave a first rate performance in: *Three Comrades*; *The Pied Piper*; *Life Begins at 8:30*; *Since You Went Away*; *Irish Eyes Are Smiling*; *Molly and Me*; *Night and Day*; *The Bishop's Wife*; *Miss Tatlock's Millions*; and *As Young as You Feel*. Woolley died May 6, 1963 in an Albany Hospital.

Monty Woolley, left, with Constance Bennett in *As Young As You Feel*.

Joe Yule, right, with Renie Riano in *Jiggs and Maggie in Jackpot Jitters.*

Joe Yule
1894-1950

Joe Yule had one distinction no other actor could claim. He was the father of Mickey Rooney. He was born in Scotland April 30, 1894. He began his career as a dead-end kid in *The Child Slaves of New York*. For twenty-three years he was a burlesque entertainer and played in melodramas and with stock companies. His first wife, Nell Carter, and Rooney's mother, were a vaudeville team until 1930. Yule signed an M-G-M contract in 1938 and appeared in: *Idiot's Delight; Sudden Money; Fast and Furious; The Secret of Dr. Kildare; Judge Hardy and Son; Broadway Melody of 1940* and *Boom Town*. In 1948 he was chosen to play the pudgy, pug-nosed comic strip character "Jiggs" in several Jiggs and Maggie films. Veteran character actress Renie Riano played "Maggie." He died March 30, 1959 of a heart attack.